Émile Zola: A Very Short Introduction

VERY SHORT INTRODUCTIONS are for anyone wanting a stimulating and accessible way into a new subject. They are written by experts, and have been translated into more than 45 different languages.

The series began in 1995, and now covers a wide variety of topics in every discipline. The VSI library currently contains over 650 volumes—a Very Short Introduction to everything from Psychology and Philosophy of Science to American History and Relativity—and continues to grow in every subject area.

Very Short Introductions available now:

ABOLITIONISM Richard S. Newman
THE ABRAHAMIC RELIGIONS
   Charles L. Cohen
ACCOUNTING Christopher Nobes
ADAM SMITH Christopher J. Berry
ADOLESCENCE Peter K. Smith
ADVERTISING Winston Fletcher
AERIAL WARFARE Frank Ledwidge
AESTHETICS Bence Nanay
AFRICAN AMERICAN RELIGION
   Eddie S. Glaude Jr
AFRICAN HISTORY John Parker and
   Richard Rathbone
AFRICAN POLITICS Ian Taylor
AFRICAN RELIGIONS
   Jacob K. Olupona
AGEING Nancy A. Pachana
AGNOSTICISM Robin Le Poidevin
AGRICULTURE Paul Brassley and
   Richard Soffe
ALBERT CAMUS Oliver Gloag
ALEXANDER THE GREAT
   Hugh Bowden
ALGEBRA Peter M. Higgins
AMERICAN CULTURAL HISTORY
   Eric Avila
AMERICAN FOREIGN RELATIONS
   Andrew Preston
AMERICAN HISTORY Paul S. Boyer
AMERICAN IMMIGRATION
   David A. Gerber
AMERICAN LEGAL HISTORY
   G. Edward White
AMERICAN NAVAL HISTORY
   Craig L. Symonds

AMERICAN POLITICAL HISTORY
   Donald Critchlow
AMERICAN POLITICAL PARTIES
   AND ELECTIONS L. Sandy Maisel
AMERICAN POLITICS
   Richard M. Valelly
THE AMERICAN PRESIDENCY
   Charles O. Jones
THE AMERICAN REVOLUTION
   Robert J. Allison
AMERICAN SLAVERY
   Heather Andrea Williams
THE AMERICAN WEST
   Stephen Aron
AMERICAN WOMEN'S HISTORY
   Susan Ware
ANAESTHESIA Aidan O'Donnell
ANALYTIC PHILOSOPHY
   Michael Beaney
ANARCHISM Colin Ward
ANCIENT ASSYRIA Karen Radner
ANCIENT EGYPT Ian Shaw
ANCIENT EGYPTIAN ART AND
   ARCHITECTURE Christina Riggs
ANCIENT GREECE Paul Cartledge
THE ANCIENT NEAR EAST
   Amanda H. Podany
ANCIENT PHILOSOPHY Julia Annas
ANCIENT WARFARE
   Harry Sidebottom
ANGELS David Albert Jones
ANGLICANISM Mark Chapman
THE ANGLO-SAXON AGE John Blair
ANIMAL BEHAVIOUR
   Tristram D. Wyatt

Available soon:

For more information visit our website

www.oup.com/vsi/

Brian Nelson

ÉMILE ZOLA

A Very Short Introduction

OXFORD
UNIVERSITY PRESS

OXFORD
UNIVERSITY PRESS

Great Clarendon Street, Oxford, OX2 6DP,
United Kingdom

Oxford University Press is a department of the University of Oxford.
It furthers the University's objective of excellence in research, scholarship,
and education by publishing worldwide. Oxford is a registered trade mark of
Oxford University Press in the UK and in certain other countries

Published in the United States of America by Oxford University Press
198 Madison Avenue, New York, NY 10016, United States of America

British Library Cataloguing in Publication Data
Data available

Library of Congress Control Number: 2020934975

ISBN 978–0–19–883756–5

Printed in Great Britain by
Ashford Colour Press Ltd, Gosport, Hampshire

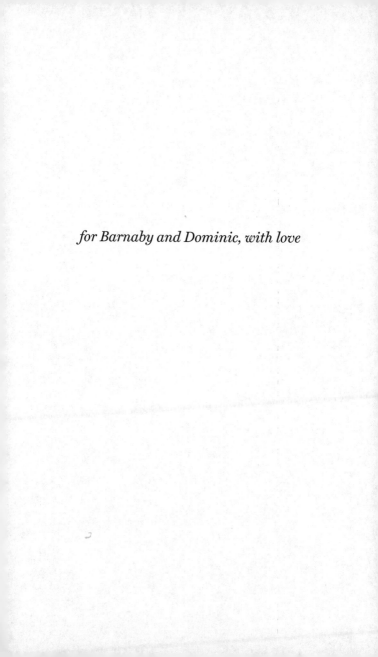

for Barnaby and Dominic, with love

Contents

Acknowledgements

I have drawn extensively in this book on the introductions I have written to my (and others') translations of Zola novels for Oxford World's Classics, and it gives me great pleasure to pay tribute to my editors at Oxford. I am especially grateful to Judith Luna for her advice and encouragement. Thanks are also due to Luciana O'Flaherty, Kizzy Taylor-Richelieu, Jenny Nugee, Andrea Keegan, Rowena Anketell, Chandrakala Chandrasekaran, and Dorothy McCarthy. Friends and colleagues whose support I warmly acknowledge include Rosemary Lloyd, Valerie Minogue, Tim Unwin, and Ilona Chessid. My thanks go too to the Brown Foundation in Houston for a Fellowship that enabled me to spend a month at the Dora Maar House in Ménerbes, France, where I completed this book in one of the most pleasant working environments imaginable. Finally, I wish to express my deep appreciation of the work of Henri Mitterand, doyen of Zola studies for the last sixty years. The debt to him of all *zolistes* is incalculable.

List of illustrations

Introduction

Émile Zola wrote thirty-one novels, five collections of short stories, a large body of art, drama, and literary criticism, several plays and libretti, and a prodigious number of articles on political and social issues during his career, from 1865 until 1881, as a journalist ('the greatest journalist of the nineteenth century', according to Anita Brookner). His main literary achievement was his twenty-volume novel cycle *Les Rougon-Macquart* (1871–93), which established his reputation as a major figure in the history of French fiction. In this cycle he set out to examine methodically, in an almost encyclopedic way, the society of his time. The fortunes of a family, the Rougon-Macquarts, are followed over several decades. The various family members spread throughout all levels of society, and through their lives Zola examines the changing cultural landscape of the late 19th century (which is still, in many ways, our society), creating an epic sense of social transformation. Zola is the quintessential novelist of modernity, understood as a time of dynamic change. The motor of change was the growth of industrial capitalism, with all that it entailed in terms of the new shapes of the city, new forms of social practice and economic organization, and heightened political pressures. Zola was fascinated by change, and specifically by the emergence of mass society. One of the most innovative aspects of his work was his portrayal of crowds—on the boulevards, in the streets, in a department store, in a tenement building, in an apartment block, in a mining village, at the stock exchange, at the theatre.

As the Rougon-Macquart project unfolded, Zola opened the novel up to a new realm of subjects: the reality of urban poverty, class consciousness and class relations, questions of sexuality and gender. Moreover, his writing embodied a new freedom of expression in their depiction. The overt sexual content of some of his novels, and the explicit language he used to describe the female body, shocked many of his early readers (especially in Victorian Britain, where the translations produced by the publisher Henry Vizetelly (1820–94) led to a heated debate in the House of Commons during which Zola's novels were condemned as representing a grave threat to public morality; in 1888 Vizetelly was convicted of obscenity and imprisoned for three months). As for the working class, *L'Assommoir* (1877) was the first novel to represent how the workers really lived, while *Germinal* (1885) showed how the labour movement had become a radically new element in French society.

'All my life,' Zola wrote in his *Letter to France* of 7 January 1898, 'I have had but one passion: the truth.' His commitment to the value of 'truth' meant a commitment to integrity both as a human quality and as an aesthetic principle. In the latter sense (integrity of representation), it means 'telling it how it is', including the belief that no aspect of human experience is out of bounds. Zola's emphasis on speaking the truth, and his innovative subject matter, were based on his conviction that the writer must play a social role. In particular, he wished to represent the sorts of things that impinged on the lives of ordinary people, such as the growth of the city, the abuse of power, the birth of consumer culture, the workings of the banking system, crime, poverty, prostitution. And he wrote about these things not dispassionately, in a documentary manner, but ironically and satirically. As Al Alvarez has argued, all enduring works of literature begin and end with the writer's voice (as distinct from his/her style). Zola's voice is challenging, combative, critical. At every stage of his life he was involved in controversy. As a journalist, he championed Manet and the Impressionists against the upholders of academic art; he was an outspoken critic of the Second Empire; and he attacked the stuffy moral conservatism of the early years of the Third Republic. As a novelist, he founded the naturalist school in opposition to the literature of Good Taste: there was the shock of *Thérèse Raquin* (1867), the scandal of *L'Assommoir* (1877), the provocation of *Nana* (1880), the warning of *Germinal* (1885), the brutality of *Earth* (1887), the critique of organized religion in *Three Cities* (1894–8).

The subversive impact of Zola's work can be measured by the extent to which he was attacked by establishment critics. He was the most maligned as well as the most popular writer of his day. The criticisms of him were usually cast in moral and aesthetic terms. He was routinely condemned for vulgarity and a morbid obsession with 'filth'. The graphic language of his novels was often cited as the reason for his repeated rejection (on nineteen occasions) by the country's most elite literary institution, the Académie française. He never stopped being a danger to the established order. He was consciously, and increasingly, a public writer. It was entirely appropriate that in 1898 he crowned his literary career with a political act: 'J'accuse!', his famous open letter to the President of the Republic in defence of Alfred Dreyfus, the Jewish army officer falsely accused of treason.

Zola dubbed his brand of realism 'naturalism' to reinforce his image as a new, serious kind of novelist whose work was aligned with science. His promotion of the pseudo-scientific theories he expounded in his essay *The Experimental Novel* (1880) and elsewhere was unremitting. Unfortunately, this helped to foster the deeply misleading notion that his writing was virtually non-literary. It encouraged people to read his novels on the basis of his theoretical writings rather than in terms of the texts themselves: in terms of their formal characteristics and effects.

3

It is still necessary, even now, to stress that Zola is above all a narrative artist: a craftsman, a storyteller, a fabulist. It is the lyrical and mythopoeic qualities of his work, and the sheer energy and inventiveness of his writing, that make him one of the great figures of the European novel.

Chapter 1
Zola and the art of fiction

Zola was a very methodical writer. This reflected in part his 'scientific' conception of his art, based on the twin principles of 'observation' and 'experimentation'. Beginning with *The Belly of Paris* (*Le Ventre de Paris*, 1873), the writing of each novel was preceded by a period of preparation and research that resulted in a set of thick dossiers. These 'planning notes' ('dossiers préparatoires') all follow a similar pattern. There is an *Ébauche* (Outline), a loose set of preliminary notes in which the novelist gives a broad-brush indication of the themes, setting, plot, and main characters of the novel in question. In a section entitled 'Characters' he draws up a file on each character, giving their main biographical, physical, and psychological particulars. A section entitled 'Plans' usually includes a brief summary and two series of detailed plans in which he organizes the narrative and descriptive material chapter by chapter. Finally, there is a section containing documentation based on his reading notes and, often, his fieldwork. The fieldwork involved not only interviews with 'experts' but also the exploration of reality itself. Researching *Germinal* (1885), for instance, he took his notebook down a mine, pretending to be an engineer visiting the coal mines of northern France. He combined the approach of the investigative reporter with that of the sociologist in his observation of the modes of existence of particular milieux.

The poetry of fact

The research notes Zola assembled for each novel represent a remarkable stock of documentary information about French society in the 1870s and 1880s. The ethnographer coexists, however, with the creative writer. Zola's fiction acquires its power, not from its ethnographic richness but from its imaginative qualities. One of the most important critical trends in France in recent years has been 'genetic criticism' (that is, the study of the creative process through an examination of the 'avant-texte': a writer's notes, sketches, drafts, manuscripts, proofs, and correspondence). As applied to Zola, such criticism has shown how the writer's planning notes, far from illustrating the naturalist method he extolled with such polemical zeal, reveal the paramount role of the imagination. The eminent Zola scholar Henri Mitterand has demonstrated how the story and characters existed before Zola began his documentation, and were shaped by pre-existing literary models and stereotypes: narrative patterns such as the struggle between the Fat (the complacent petty bourgeois supporters of the Second Empire) and the Thin (the political idealists or artists) in *The Belly of Paris*, stock figures like the good worker and the bad worker in *L'Assommoir*, dramatic scenes like the knife fight between Coupeau and Lantier planned for the ending of *L'Assommoir*. Similarly, documentary research was generally dictated by the needs of the fiction: when Zola visited a particular location or consulted a book, he already knew what he was looking for and to what end.

The art criticism Zola wrote during the late 1860s shows his clear awareness that 'observation' is not an unproblematic process; he recognizes the importance of the observer in the act of observation. But in his writings on his naturalist theories during the 1870s, he said relatively little about his narrative art, preferring to ignore or downplay that aspect of his work. His propaganda for the 'experimental novel' was so successful in reinforcing his image as a new kind of novelist with little time for mere invention, that the formal qualities of his writing, especially its poetic character, were obscured. What makes Zola's best novels compelling is their visionary power, their mythic resonance, their movement, colour, and intensity. The hallmarks of his work are his compositional skill, his control of narrative rhythm, his brilliant treatment of physical settings (especially urban spaces), his remarkable use of metaphor, the expressive value of his descriptions. His famous long descriptions are not mechanical products of his naturalist credo, simple 'copies' of the real; rather, they express the very meaning, and critical dimension, of his narratives. The descriptions in *The Kill* (*La Curée*, 1872) of the luxurious physical decor of bourgeois existence—houses, interiors, social gatherings—are marked syntactically by the eclipse of human subjects by abstract nouns and things, expressing a vision of a society which, organized under the aegis of the commodity, turns people into objects. Similarly, the descriptions of the sales in *The Ladies' Paradise* (*Au Bonheur des Dames*, 1883), with their cascading images and rising pitch, suggest loss of control, the female shoppers' quasi-sexual abandonment to consumer dreams, while mirroring the perpetual expansion that defines the economic principles of consumerism. Through the play of imagery and metaphor, Zola magnifies the material world, giving it a hyperbolic, hallucinatory quality. We think of Saccard, the protagonist of *The Kill*, swimming in a sea of gold coins; the fantastic visions of food in *The Belly of Paris*; Nana's mansion (*Nana*, 1880), swallowing up men and their fortunes; the pithead in *Germinal*, rising spectrally out of the darkness.

Symbol, allegory, myth

In a letter to his disciple Henry Céard dated 22 March 1885, just after the publication of *Germinal*, Zola wrote:

We all falsify more or less, but…I think I falsify in the direction of truth. I have a hypertrophic desire for authentic detail; the springboard of precise observation makes possible the leap towards the stars. Truth wings its way to the symbol.

No symbol plays a more central role in Zola's imaginary world than the machine. Many of Zola's novels are organized round a machine (for example, the distilling machine in *L'Assommoir* and the locomotive in *The Beast Within* (*La Bête humaine*, 1890)) or an entity that functions like a machine (the food markets in *The Belly of Paris*, the department store in *The Ladies' Paradise*, the coal mine in *Germinal*, the stock exchange in *Money* (*L'Argent*, 1891)). These emblematic features of contemporary life are used as giant symbols of industrial modernity and of the forces and pressures circulating within it. Zola sees allegories of contemporary life everywhere. In *The Kill* the new city under construction becomes a vast symbol of the corruption, as well as the dynamism, of Second Empire society. In *The Ladies' Paradise* the department store is emblematic of the new dream world of consumer culture and of the changes in sexual attitudes and class relations taking place at the time.

Zola wished to demonstrate the ways in which human behaviour is determined by environment and heredity. However, heredity serves in his novels not simply as a scientific theme but as a structuring device, analogous to the use of recurring characters in the fiction of Honoré de Balzac (1799–1850); and it also has great dramatic force, allowing the novelist to give a mythic dimension to his representation of the human condition. In terms of his characters, many of them are 'ordinary' (naturalistic) working-class or bourgeois figures; but others, while located in the historical reality of the Second Empire, are also rooted in myth. As Chantal Pierre-Gnassounou writes:

> Many of Zola's characters originate not from a familiar modernity but from a sort of original chaos, in which sex, blood and murder—Eros and Thanatos—intermingle. In this sense, the character of Jacques Lantier, the murderer in *La Bête humaine*,

haunted by obsessive images of rape and murder, brings to the surface the archaic substratum that is the basis of most of Zola's heroes. His heredity links him, beyond the generations of alcoholics, with the primal horde, and the Dionysian era Nietzsche speaks of in *The Birth of Tragedy* (1872).

Zola uses heredity selectively, to serve his aesthetic purposes, evoking it to create a sense of doom, like an ancient curse. Adélaïde Fouque (Tante Dide), the mad ancestress who features in *The Fortune of the Rougons* (*La Fortune des Rougon*, 1871), is the origin of that curse, the flawed heredity that turns the Rougon-Macquart family into a latter-day equivalent of the House of Atreus in Greek mythology. Similarly, the protagonists of *The Belly of Paris* enact the story of the eternal struggle between the Fat and the Thin; Goujet, the giant metal worker of *L'Assommoir*, is presented as a modern Titan; Nana first appears to us on the stage of a variety theatre as Venus, prefiguring her future as a 'man-eater'; Étienne Lantier, in *Germinal*, becomes Theseus, set in conflict with the Minotaur of the mine.

Mythopoeic vision informs Zola's imagination not simply in terms of parallels between certain characters and figures from classical (or biblical) mythology; it also informs the basic narrative patterns of his novels. There is the origin myth of the first novel of the series, *The Fortune of the Rougons*; the myths of hell and the universal flood in *Germinal*; the myth of the Garden of Eden and the Tree of Knowledge in *The Sin of Father Mouret* (*La Faute de l'abbé Mouret*, 1875); the myth of Man's lost majesty in *The Sin of Father Mouret* and *L'Assommoir*; the myth of the Eternal Return in *Earth*; the myths of Catastrophe and Renewal in the later novels of *Les Rougon-Macquart*, from *Nana* onwards.

The remarkable fusion of naturalistic and poetic modes in Zola should make readers aware of the complexity and pliancy of the labels 'realism' and 'naturalism'. Since the 1950s academic criticism of all kinds, by bringing out the poetic and visionary aspects of Zola's novels, has done much to undermine stereotypes of him as a sensationalist writer fond of squalor and violence, or a stolid producer of novels that relied more on documentation than the creative imagination. Reductive readings of his work have been further undermined in recent years by critics who have drawn attention to the surprising ways in which his work prefigures themes and textual strategies of modernist literature. An important critical study in this regard is Susan Harrow's *Zola, The Body Modern: Pressures and Prospects of Representation*. Harrow shows how Zola's descriptions often anticipate the surrealism of writers like Louis Aragon (1897–1982) and André Breton (1896–1966), while his frequent use of reflexivity (that is, the reflection of the work within the work) links him with 20th-century modernism. For example, the railway line in *La Bête humaine* becomes a metaphor for the narrative system itself. It is possible to read Zola as an 'experimental' novelist in ways that have nothing to do with the theories he expounded in his *Experimental Novel* essay of 1880.

Chapter 2
Before the *Rougon-Macquart*

Zola was born in Paris—in the Rue Saint-Joseph, not far from the Bourse (the Paris stock exchange)—on 2 April 1840. He was the only child of Francesco Zolla (later François Zola) and Émilie Aubert, who had married the previous year. Émilie, twenty-four years younger than her husband, came from a working-class family, originally from Dourdan, a small town near Chartres. Francesco, 44 at the time of his marriage, was a brilliant and enterprising civil engineer. As his name implies, he was Italian (Zola himself, as a consequence of his parentage, did not become a French citizen until the age of 21).

In the 1830s Francesco established himself in Marseilles, with an office on the Canebière. For several years he fought to obtain a contract for the construction of a new dockyard connected to the Vieux Port, which had become too small for the increased maritime traffic flowing from the opening up of North Africa. In the end, the commission was granted to a rival. He submitted to the government an equally bold plan, for the fortification of Paris; but this also fell through. It was during one of his numerous trips to Paris that he met Émilie Aubert. Indomitable as ever, he had already conceived a new scheme: to build a dam and canal that would bring fresh water to Aix-en-Provence, which was threatened every summer with drought. With the help of the statesman Adolphe Thiers, a native of the area, he succeeded in securing royal approval for the scheme, and in 1843 moved with his wife and child to Aix. In February 1847, after protracted negotiations with the local authorities and landowners, work began. While supervising his workmen in the mountains Francesco caught a chill, but insisted on travelling on to Marseilles where he had urgent business to attend to. Here he fell seriously ill with pneumonia and, at the age of 51, died in his hotel room.

Francesco's death occurred less than a week before Émile's seventh birthday. It deeply affected the boy. Moreover, the Zola household now found itself quite impoverished. This led Zola's mother to embark on an ultimately fruitless decade of legal wranglings with the Société du Canal Zola in an attempt to keep the modest annuity they paid her and receive due compensation for her shares. The family moved from their big house in the Impasse Sylvacane, in the bourgeois quarter, to a series of smaller lodgings, and finally to a workman's cottage. These years undoubtedly toughened Zola's character, gave him a keen sense of justice, and made him realize that later in life he would have to depend on his own efforts alone.

His feelings towards Aix (which became the Plassans of his fiction and is described in detail in *The Fortune of the Rougons*) were highly ambivalent. He resented the family's equivocal social position, but he loved the town itself and the Provençal countryside. His mother (and her parents, who had come to live in Aix) provided him with a protective home environment, and his schooling seems to have been relatively happy. He attended the Pension Notre-Dame; and then, from 1852, the Collège Bourbon (now the Collège Mignet), a Jesuit school where Aix notables and rich farmers sent their children. A bursary was secured for him by a friend of his father, Alexandre Labot. To begin with, he found it hard to adapt. The Zolas were regarded as outsiders by the local population, and Émile's classmates teased him for his slight lisp and his Parisian accent. But he did well academically, winning a number of prizes. Also, he formed close friendships, most notably with two slightly older boys: Paul Cézanne, the future painter, and Jean-Baptistin Baille, who would become a professor of optics and acoustics in Paris. The friendship with Cézanne was to last nearly thirty years.

In November 1857 Madame Aubert, Zola's grandmother, died. In December Zola's mother moved back to Paris, having decided to cut her losses in Aix and see whether any of her husband's former associates in Paris could help her. In February of the following year, Émile and his grandfather joined her in the furnished lodgings she had taken in a tenement house at 63, Rue Monsieur-le-Prince, in the Latin Quarter. Madame Zola, concerned to make the best possible arrangements for Émile's education, had again enlisted the help of Alexandre Labot, with the result that Émile was awarded a bursary to attend the prestigious Lycée Saint-Louis as a day-boy. He felt ill at ease among the sons of the prosperous bourgeoisie, and began to struggle academically. In November he fell seriously ill with typhoid fever, and for a while was delirious. It took him weeks to recover. He was to draw on this experience when he described the illness and delirium of Serge Mouret in *The Sin of Abbé Mouret*. In 1859 he failed his *baccalauréat* twice. Unable to enter any of the liberal professions, and under increasing financial pressure, he began to look around for a job. Once more, Labot came to his aid and in April 1860 found him a position as copy clerk in the Excise Office of the Paris Docks, near the Canal Saint-Martin. After three months of mind-numbing work, he gave it up and withdrew into a 'bohemian' existence. He saw himself as a Romantic poet in the tradition of Lamartine, Hugo, and Musset.

His letters to Cézanne and Baille during this period reveal his fascination with literature and art, his dreams of a literary career, and his absolute determination to succeed. However, he had virtually no money, was forced to borrow from friends, and lived in extreme poverty. He was repeatedly evicted for failing to pay his rent, moving six times on the Left Bank between 1858 and 1862.

He nearly starved; but he read voraciously (Michelet, Sand, Montaigne, Molière, and Shakespeare, as well as the Romantic poets), wrote copious amounts of poetry, frequented artists' studios, and became immersed in the lower-class worlds of the city, which was then in the throes of Baron Haussmann's urban redevelopment programme (Box 1).

The winter of 1861–2 was especially hard. He was living in a kind of doss-house in the Rue Soufflot, near the Panthéon, which at that time was in the middle of a slum area; the house was used by students and prostitutes (Zola himself became involved with a

Box 1 The remaking of Paris by Baron Haussmann

To establish his authority and to glorify his rule, Louis-Napoleon Bonaparte (Napoleon III) pursued a policy of modernization through a monumental scheme of urban redevelopment. He entrusted this project to Georges Eugène Haussmann (1809–91), whom he appointed Prefect of the Seine (in effect, chief administrator of Paris). The term *Haussmanisation* began to be used to denote the transformation of the city. Throughout the 1850s and 1860s the overcrowded central areas were demolished, and a system of rectilinear boulevards—notably the Boulevards de Strasbourg, de Sébastopol, Saint-Michel, and Saint-Germain—was constructed, binding the city together as a single structural entity. The devastation of *vieux Paris*, and the various communities within it, was deeply controversial, but Baron Haussmann (as he called himself) pursued his renovations relentlessly. At the height of the fever of reconstruction, one in five Parisian workers was employed in the building trade. Real-estate speculation (vividly depicted by Zola in *The Kill*) became all the rage. Large sections of the working class were forced into cheaper outlying areas, dividing Paris into a preponderantly middle- and upper-class west and a working-class east (Belleville, Ménilmontant, La Chapelle, La Villette).

prostitute named Berthe), and was frequently subject to police raids (of a kind evoked in *Nana*). The descriptions of poverty in *L'Assommoir* have an intensity derived in part from intimate personal knowledge.

Apprenticeship

In March 1861 Zola's luck changed: he was taken on at the rapidly expanding publishing house of Hachette. This was to provide him with an invaluable apprenticeship in the world of books, writing, and contemporary ideas.

At Hachette's (situated at the corner of the Boulevard Saint-Michel and the Boulevard Saint-Germain) Zola began by working in the post room, packing books. Within four months, however, he sent Louis Hachette a memorandum suggesting the launch of a magazine, to be called the *Bibliothèque des débutants*, which would print the work of young, up-and-coming writers. Impressed by Zola's initiative, Hachette put him in charge of sales promotion and doubled his salary. As head of publicity, Zola's job was to compose advertising copy for new books and induce reviewers to give them favourable notices. His dealings with reviewers, authors, and the literary editors of newspapers opened his eyes to the string-pulling and back-scratching that went into the building of literary reputations. It seemed that the art of self-promotion was almost as important as talent.

He lost no time in putting these lessons into practice. When his first book, a collection of romantic tales entitled *Tales for Ninon* (*Contes à Ninon*), was published by Pierre Hetzel and his partner Albert Lacroix in November 1864, he wrote his own 'blurb', sent it to all the newspaper editors he could count on for a friendly reaction, and even offered to provide them with a review written by 'a friend' which they could use gratis. The volume was duly given an indulgent reception. A similar publicity campaign accompanied his second published work, *Claude's Confession*

(*La Confession de Claude*, 1865), a semi-autobiographical novel based on his failed attempt to reclaim the prostitute Berthe. It attracted the attention of the public prosecutor, who declared that the novel was in very bad taste but decided that there was no case for prosecution, given the book's moralistic intention.

The publicity over *Claude's Confession* was not considered desirable by Zola's employers at Hachette, and in January 1866 he resigned, determined to make a living by his pen alone. By this time a woman had entered his life: a tall, handsome brunette named Alexandrine-Gabrielle Meley, who would become his wife in 1870. A year older than Zola, she was the illegitimate daughter of an 18-year-old hatter and an even younger florist. Her early years were difficult. She was always reluctant to talk about her past, which remains obscure. We do know that at the age of 19 she was seduced and deserted, gave birth to a daughter, and, like thousands of young women at the time, handed her over to the local foundling hospital. The baby died soon afterwards. Alexandrine was devoted to Zola and gave him a much-needed sense of security.

On leaving Hachette, Zola became a contributor to a new daily newspaper, *L'Événement*, which had been launched in November 1865 by Hippolyte de Villemessant, one of the most enterprising proprietors of the period. Villemessant paid Zola 500 francs a month, two and a half times his salary at Hachette's. He had been much taken by an idea Zola had put to him the previous year, involving the use of his contacts in the publishing world. The proposal was a kind of literary gossip column featuring books that were about to appear, and including extracts taken from the galley proofs. In February 1866 Zola embarked on this new project.

Manet and the 'Salon des Refusés'

Though fully immersed in the literary world, he was now spending more and more time in the company of painters. Cézanne had spent a few unhappy months in Paris in 1861, but had returned in 1862. He introduced Zola to the landscape painter Antoine Guillemet, and the two artists took their friend round the studios, introducing him to Frédéric Bazille, Claude Monet, Camille Pissarro, and Auguste Renoir.

In February 1866 Guillemet took Zola to the Café Guerbois, on the Avenue de Clichy in the Batignolles district of Paris. This was becoming a regular meeting-place not just for young avant-garde artists but for critics sympathetic to their cause, such as the novelist Edmond Duranty, who had championed the realist movement in literature during the 1850s. The painters who gathered there were coming to be known as the 'Batignolles School'. Zola listened avidly to their discussions, of which a prominent motif was the annual 'Salon', held at the Palais de l'Industrie, for which artists submitted paintings to a jury controlled by the official art world embodied in the Académie des Beaux-Arts. The jury selected the paintings they considered worthy of exhibition. Large crowds were drawn to these Salons, and, in the absence of private art galleries as we know them today, it was an important step in an artist's career to have a painting chosen for exhibition. The Batignolles artists were continually rejected by the jury. The sticking point was the type of art it was felt appropriate to encourage and celebrate. The poet Charles Baudelaire, in his celebrated essay *The Painter of Modern Life* (*Le Peintre de la vie moderne*, 1863), argued that if art was to be relevant, it had to concern itself with the contemporary world, and could no longer be limited to the conventional types of painting exhibited at the Salon every year: scenes from ancient history, mythology, the Bible, and so on. Modern beauty, Baudelaire declared, was to be found in contemporary urban existence, and was diametrically opposed to the 'timeless' themes of the classical tradition as well as to the Romantic cult of nature.

The Salon of 1863 had refused more than half of the 5,000 submissions. As a gesture of appeasement, the government and art establishment offered an exhibition space at the Palais des Champs-Élysées for the rejected works. Not surprisingly, this so-called Salon des Refusés (Salon of the Rejected) immediately became a kind of counter-establishment exhibition. Ridicule was heaped on the participating artists in the popular press, and the public came to scoff.

The main focus of derision was Édouard Manet's *Le Déjeuner sur l'herbe* (*Lunch on the Grass*; see Figure 1), which depicted a nude woman in the company of two fully dressed young men. The subject was provocative, and the direct, unblinking gaze of the woman was immediately confronting. But what really disconcerted the critics was the fact that Manet had based the composition of his central group of figures on an engraving after Raphael's *Judgement of Paris* and transformed the traditional theme of *la fête champêtre* ('pastoral interlude') into a modern idiom, replacing an idyllic and safely mythological setting with one that depicted picnickers who

1. **Édouard Manet,** *Le Déjeuner sur l'herbe* (*Lunch on the Grass*)**, 1863.**

were clearly recognizable as contemporaries of the spectators. When Napoleon III saw *Le Déjeuner sur l'herbe* at the Salon, he said it was 'an offence against decency'; while, apparently, the Empress Eugénie pretended that the picture did not exist.

In 1865 Manet caused an even greater scandal, this time with a painting that was accepted by the Salon, *Olympia*. Again, the painting alluded ironically to art of the past, this time to Titian's *Venus of Urbino*. Manet replaced the goddess of love with a contemporary courtesan with a challenging gaze, transforming the classical theme of the idealized female nude into an image of what had become an important facet of modern Parisian life. Manet's critics were greatly perturbed to see a mythological figure, closely attached to an academic tradition that was deeply embedded in government institutions, transformed so provocatively into a commentary on current society.

Zola was caught up in the enthusiasm of the young painters for their iconoclastic ideas, and shared their contempt for the arch-conservatism of the art establishment. Indeed, he identified with them, seeing them as seekers after truth in their representation of the scenes or people they painted. He appreciated their courage to innovate, to express their own temperaments, in defiance of current conventions. He dubbed them 'realists' by virtue of their desire to engage with contemporary reality.

Art criticism

Already controversial because of his outspoken literary criticism and his skirmish with the public prosecutor over *Claude's Confession*, Zola now saw an opportunity to gain new notoriety as an art critic. He asked Villemessant to let him write a review of the 1866 Salon, from which the Batignolles painters had again been excluded. As was customary, the review would consist of a series of articles penned over several weeks.

The Salon traditionally opened on 1 May. To steal a march on his fellow critics, Zola published the first two articles in his series at the end of April. With calculated impertinence, he began: 'Before passing judgement on the artists admitted to exhibit, it seems only right that I should begin by passing judgement on the judges.' He condemned their cliquishness, corruption, and conservatism. In his third article he expounded his view that what made a work of art was its expression of the creator's individual temperament. His fourth article was devoted to Manet. By excluding him from the Salon, he argued, the establishment was making him pay for the impudence of *Olympia*. He declared that Manet was a master whose rightful place was in the Louvre. In his fifth article, 'Les réalistes du Salon', he wrote: 'The wind is blowing in the direction of science; we are driven, despite ourselves, towards the exact study of facts and things.' The sixth article dealt with three established artists, Gustave Courbet, Jean-François Millet, and Théodore Rousseau, whose paintings at this Salon had, in Zola's opinion, lost the vitality of their earlier works.

Zola's articles (published as a slim volume entitled *Mon Salon* in July 1866) caused a sensation. Villemessant was inundated with letters of protest, and a number of readers of *L'Événement* cancelled their subscriptions. Villemessant told his art critic to wind up his series. In his valedictory article ('Adieux d'un critique d'art'), Zola reiterated his ideas on what he looked for in a painting and upheld his defence of Manet, declaring: 'I will always be on the side of the underdog. There will always be conflict between indomitable temperaments and the crowd.' There could hardly be any doubt, at the end of this remarkable campaign, about Zola's own indomitable temperament and the fact that he had truly found his 'voice': outspoken, provocative, anti-establishment.

Zola's friends at the Café Guerbois were delighted to receive the help he had so effectively given them. Manet wrote to thank Zola

2. Édouard Manet, *Portrait of Émile Zola*, 1865.

for his support and expressed his desire to get to know him better.
He also lent him money and, as a gesture of gratitude, painted his
portrait. The portrait (now on display at the Musée d'Orsay in
Paris) was exhibited at the 1868 Salon. On the wall behind Zola is
a reproduction of Manet's *Olympia*. With characteristic wit,
Manet shows her with her eyes turned towards her admirer

(see Figure 2). Zola's long essay on Manet in January 1867 in the *Revue du XIXe siècle*, 'A New Way to Paint: Édouard Manet', published as a brochure later that year, consolidated his reputation as champion of the 'new painting'. Zola's defence of Manet and the painters who were soon to become known by the collective name of Impressionists was historically important; and contemporary painting, its theorizing and its practices, was a powerful factor in the shaping of Zola's own aesthetic. His contact with painters also had a profound influence on his art in terms of visual effects, compositional techniques, and choice of motifs:

> the open-air dance hall, the laundress (Degas), the actress, the theatre scene, crowds on the boulevard, still lifes in the market, station platforms, the Seine (Guillemet, Degas, Manet, Monet), the races (Degas), waves (Manet, Courbet), the swing (Renoir, Cézanne, Manet)…Taine taught Zola a system of thought. But it was Zola's friends, Chaillan, Cézanne, Bazille, Manet, Pissarro, Renoir, and Fantin-Latour, who taught him to look at modern life and to look at it with the eye of a painter, skilled in capturing the interplay of forms, colours, movements, and light effects.

Materialist vision and the cult of science

The terms of Zola's articles for *L'Événement*—his reference to the prestige of science and 'the exact study of facts and things'—clearly indicate that he was shedding his youthful Romanticism and developing an aesthetic of realism. This tendency was made abundantly clear in *Mes Haines* (*My Hatreds*, 1866), a selection of articles he had contributed to *Le Salut public*. He wrote in high praise of the realist novelist Balzac and the critical method of Hippolyte Taine (1828–93), the literary historian and critic whose radically materialist views had a profound influence on him.

During the third quarter of the 19th century, industrialization in France accelerated, while scientific discoveries were constantly converted into inventions and processes that began to transform everyday life (for example, the steam engine, the locomotive, electricity, the vaccines developed by Louis Pasteur, 1822–95). The cult of science underlay most 19th-century social theories, and predicated a universe governed by laws which, when grasped, would reveal the 'truth' about the nature of man and his place in the world. In philosophy the scientific method bred positivism, expounded by Auguste Comte (1798–1857) in his six-volume *Cours de philosophie positive* (1830–42). Comte believed that 'truth' was arrived at, not through metaphysical ideas derived from man's consciousness, but through the systematic analysis of observable phenomena; we can only know what we can observe. Positivism was thus virtually anti-religious, arguing that man must shed any belief in absolute supreme causes. It was deterministic in its application of science to society; society and the universe were connected, it was argued, through the inexorable workings of changeless natural laws. And it was optimistic in its view of what scientific method could achieve: Comte believed in 'social engineering', arguing that by applying scientific method to the study of man as a social animal, and thereby deducing the laws that govern the functioning of society, it would be possible to design appropriate policies to redress social ills.

In his essay of 1880 *The Experimental Novel*, modelled on the physiologist Claude Bernard's *Introduction to the Study of Experimental Medicine*, which he had read soon after its appearance in 1865, Zola argued that the 'truth' for which he aimed could only be attained through empirical research and documentation and that his work as a novelist represented a form of practical sociology, complementing the work of the scientist; their common purpose was to improve the world by promoting greater understanding of the laws that determine the material conditions of life. The major influences shaping the individual, according to Hippolyte Taine, were 'race' (heredity), 'milieu' (environment), and 'moment' (historical context).

Advances in all branches of the sciences seemed to confirm the potential of science to reveal the seamlessness of some overarching structure of connections. The search for a unitary pattern, a master-key to an understanding of all social processes, was characteristic of much mid-19th-century thought. Karl Marx offered his contemporaries the explanatory system of the class struggle as the motor of human history. Marx's concept of the class struggle was paralleled by Charles Darwin's (1809–82) concept of the struggle for survival as the essential dynamic of human evolution.

It was in the positivistic intellectual atmosphere described above that the young Zola had found himself when he arrived in Paris in 1858. His job at Hachette's not only provided him with a platform to develop a literary career; it also brought him into contact with many leading authors, such as Taine.

Thérèse Raquin

By 1867 the thought Zola had given to the nature of realism in literature was bearing fruit; he was preparing, he wrote to Antony Valabrègue, a 'psychological and physiological novel' (letter dated 29 May 1867). It was, he felt, the best thing he had done so far. This was *Thérèse Raquin* (Figure 3), and in this novel and its preface, in which Zola used for the first time in a prominent context the term 'naturalism' to apply to the writer's art, we can see Zola's new stance towards realism and the importance he now attached to science.

Thérèse Raquin is an experiment in a new 'scientific' realism, an attempt to use scientific method via the novel to explore human psychology. Thérèse, destined by her heredity and temperament to be physically energetic and sexually passionate, represses her physical and sexual energy because of her marriage to her cousin Camille, who is temperamentally and physically her opposite. Like Manet in his paintings, Zola built his novel on brutal contrasts.

3. Publicity poster for *Thérèse Raquin*.

Thérèse enters into an affair with a friend of her husband, the virile and self-centred Laurent. When they are unable to continue their secret meetings, they begin to contemplate Camille's murder. Laurent drowns Camille, making it look like a boating accident, with Thérèse acquiescing if not physically assisting. The drowning is accepted as an accident, leaving Thérèse and Laurent free to marry. Their decision to marry, however, is the signal for both of them to experience horrifying hallucinations, all involving an appearance of Camille's corpse. Eventually they commit suicide, simultaneously, under the vengeful eye of Camille's paralysed mother, Madame Raquin, who has learnt of their guilt.

The preface to the second edition of the novel (April 1868) was written as a polemical response to the charges of immorality and pornography that had been hurled at Zola when the novel first appeared. The most ferocious of these attacks was by Louis Ulbach (under the pseudonym 'Ferragus') in an article entitled 'Putrid Literature' in *Le Figaro* of 23 January 1868. Zola's exposition of his aims begins with the statement: 'In *Thérèse Raquin* I set out to study, not characters, but temperaments.' He had chosen, he explains, two different types of temperament, one all nerves, the other entirely sanguine, and had tried to show them drawn into every act of their lives by the inexorable laws of their physical nature. They have no free will; their acts are the results of physiological and psychological dispositions exposed to certain circumstances. The novel bears the significant epigraph from Taine: 'Vice and Virtue are products like vitriol and sugar.' The adultery of the characters is simply the satisfying of a physical need, the murder is the logical consequence of the adultery, and their remorse is merely an organic disorder: 'my objective was first and foremost a scientific one...I simply carried out on two living bodies the same analytical examination that surgeons perform on corpses' (p. 3).

As Linda Nochlin has written, in terms that are particularly pertinent to Zola: 'In making truth the aim of art—truth to the facts, to perceived and experienced reality—[the Realists'] outlook evinced the same forces that shaped the scientific attitude itself.' This is indeed true; but of course, literature cannot be equated with the laboratory in any properly scientific sense. Moreover, Zola's scientific aims stick out in the text, creating a curious mixture of tones. Elements of melodrama and the fantastic are mixed with realist description and pseudo-scientific analysis. On the one hand we are asked to see the inevitable logical consequences of the situation; on the other we see everything conspiring in a world of dark foreboding, filled with fatality, dark omens, hallucinations, the silent stare of Madame Raquin and François the cat, and the working out of what seems more like an ancestral curse than a logical necessity. These atmospheric effects transcend the mechanistic view of humanity the novel was intended to embody; and it is precisely these effects that make the novel memorable. Zola creates a powerful literary narrative focused on the destructive force of sexuality.

Thérèse Raquin was not only a great popular success but also marked a crucial step in Zola's development. After its publication, he began to sketch out a plan for a series of interconnected novels. He sent the plan to his publisher, Albert Lacroix. This was the basis for *Les Rougon-Macquart*, which is subtitled 'A Natural and Social History of a Family in the Second Empire'. Conceived initially as a sequence of ten novels, the project would grow to twenty novels. Zola aimed to represent five 'worlds' (bourgeoisie, lower classes, commercial class, upper classes, and the marginal world of prostitutes, criminals, artists, and priests). His ambition, he said, was to emulate Balzac by producing an all-inclusive panorama of the contemporary world. One of the first cartoon representations of Zola is that by André Gill, in which Zola is shown saluting a bust of Balzac, who returns his salute (see Figure 4). Zola needed, of course, to distinguish his own 'human comedy' from that of Balzac; so, to link his novels together, he replaced Balzac's device of the 'recurring character' with the idea of a novel-series that would follow the fortunes of a single family

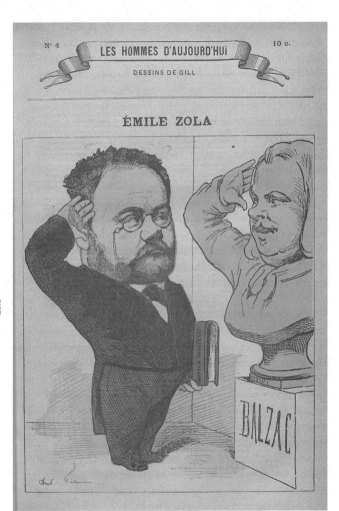

4. A comment by the cartoonist André Gill on the literary affinity between Zola and Balzac.

over several generations. This choice accorded perfectly with the 'scientific' nature of his project: to demonstrate, in a way that would reflect contemporary scientific discourse, the ways in which human behaviour is determined by heredity and environment. And he would use the symbolic possibilities of a family whose heredity is tainted with mental instability and alcoholism to represent a diseased society—the corrupt yet dynamic France of the Second Empire, the regime established on the basis of a coup d'état by Louis-Napoleon Bonaparte on 2 December 1851 and which would last until its collapse in 1870 in the face of military defeat by the Prussians at the Battle of Sedan.

The Rougon branch of the family represents the hunt for wealth and status, its members rising to commanding positions in the worlds of government and finance; the Macquarts, the illegitimate branch, are the submerged proletariat, with the exception of Lisa Macquart (*The Belly of Paris*); the Mourets, an intermediate branch springing from a marriage between cousins, are the bourgeois tradesmen and provincial bourgeoisie. Lacroix accepted Zola's proposal, and in May 1869 the author set to work on the first novel of the series, *The Fortune of the Rougons*.

Chapter 3
The fat and the thin:
The Belly of Paris

The early novels of *Les Rougon-Macquart* are strongly marked by political satire. In that sense, they reflect the 'angry young man' virulence of the articles Zola had written for the opposition newspapers *La Tribune*, *La Cloche*, and *Le Rappel* during the final years of the Second Empire. He set out in these novels to describe what he saw as the corruption and criminality of the regime, and the frenzied indulgence of appetites of every kind that it unleashed. *The Fortune of the Rougons*, subtitled 'Origins', is a novel of political intrigue and betrayal; it describes the violent beginnings of the Rougon-Macquart family as reflected in the way Pierre and Félicité Rougon turn Louis-Napoleon's coup d'état of 2 December 1851 to their own advantage. Their fortune is founded on blood: Silvère, a young republican insurgent, is executed on a tombstone by a gendarme; his murder ensures the success of the Rougons' schemes for social advancement. *The Kill* depicts the wild real-estate speculation, involving the government, that accompanied the modernization of Paris by Haussmann. The novel combines into a single vision the twin themes of 'gold' and 'flesh', lust for money and lust for pleasure. *The Belly of Paris*, the third novel of the series, exploits the metaphoric potential of food and digestion, depicting social existence as a struggle between the Fat and the Thin. Zola wrote in his planning notes

Box 2 *The Belly of Paris*: a summary

The Belly of Paris tells the story of Florent Quenu, who is walking through the streets during the disturbances provoked by Louis-Napoleon's coup d'état when soldiers start firing on the crowd. When the shooting stops, Florent tries to get up from the ground but realizes that there is a dead young woman lying on top of his legs. Some of her blood trickles onto his hands. Later that night he is arrested at a barricade and labelled dangerous, his bloody hands used as evidence of his crime. He is condemned to exile on Devil's Island (Cayenne, the notorious penal colony off the coast of French Guiana). After several years he escapes, returns to Paris, and is taken in by his half-brother Quenu and Quenu's wife Lisa. He finds the city changed beyond recognition. The old Marché des Innocents has been knocked down to make way for Les Halles, the great central food markets built by the architect Victor Baltard (1805–74). The creation of this vast glass-and-iron complex was the first big public works project of the regime; it was, in effect, a monument to the Empire's burgeoning capitalist economy. Just opposite Les Halles, in the Rue Rambuteau, the Quenus own a prosperous new *charcuterie*. Lisa tries to keep Florent's identity secret from the rest of the tradespeople, for she sees him as a troublemaker who may upset her comfortable petit-bourgeois world. At her urging, he takes a job as inspector in the fish market. After a while, he becomes involved in republican politics, leads an amateurish conspiracy against the regime, is denounced to the police by the people of the market and by Lisa, and is sentenced once more to exile. The story of Florent is that of the French 19th century, with its periodic insurrections: 1830, 1848, 1871. The bourgeois triumph repeatedly over the workers; political idealism goes nowhere.

for the novel: '*The Belly of Paris* complements *The Kill*, it is the
scramble for spoils of the middle classes, the sensual enjoyment of
rich food and undisturbed digestion ... But it portrays the same
moral and social corruption.' Though ostensibly focused on the
Second Empire, Zola's satire in this novel is also directed, indeed
more so, at contemporary society, for in many ways the new,
repressive Third Republic, proclaimed in 1870 following the fall
of Louis-Napoleon, seemed just like the Empire under a different
name (Box 2).

Background: the Commune and 'moral order'

On 19 July 1870 France declared war on Prussia. The Emperor
hoped to achieve a quick victory by marching his armies east,
straight to Berlin. Instead, the Prussian armies crossed the Rhine
first and invaded France. On 2 September, at Sedan, a whole
French army was surrounded and capitulated; Louis-Napoleon
was taken prisoner. This signified the end of the Empire. On 4
September, the Third Republic was proclaimed and the conduct
of affairs put in the hands of an emergency government. The
Prussian army continued its advance and encircled Paris. An
armistice was signed on 28 January 1871. Following elections on
8 February a new National Assembly began sitting in Bordeaux,
and Zola offered his services as parliamentary correspondent.
From 13 February to 12 March he wrote daily reports for *La
Cloche* and *Le Sémaphore de Marseille*. When the peace treaty was
signed, the Assembly moved to Versailles. The elections of
February produced an overwhelmingly conservative majority,
most of whom favoured a return to some form of monarchy. The
country as a whole wanted peace, but Paris did not. It had borne
the brunt of the four-month siege the winter before, during which
all but the most wealthy nearly starved. Parisians felt humiliated,
isolated, and betrayed by the arrangements for peace. The treaty
included conceding Alsace and Lorraine to the Prussians and the
payment of huge war reparations, which would be paid for in part
by raising taxes and interest on debts. When troops were sent to

remove the National Guard's heavy guns (which had been bought by public subscription), the city rose in revolt. A largely leaderless revolutionary government declared Paris an autonomous Commune, in emulation of the Jacobin Assembly of 1793.

Zola continued his work as parliamentary correspondent, taking the train to Versailles every morning from the Gare Saint-Lazare. He did not hide his contempt for the royalists in the Assembly, baying for the blood of the Parisian workers; but though he felt instinctive sympathy for the working-class supporters of the Commune, he had little sympathy for the revolutionary activists. At the beginning of May, reacting to arrests of Communards by the Versaillais, the newly formed Committee of Public Safety began rounding up hostages inside the city. As a journalist known to be unsympathetic to the Commune, Zola feared arrest; he took refuge for a while, with his wife and mother, in Gloton, a little village on the Seine.

The Versailles government saw the Commune as a threat to the entire social order. After a stand-off of several weeks, it determined to crush it. The regular army began to bombard Paris, and then started to close in. On 21 May began what would become known as the 'Bloody Week'. The Versailles troops forced their way into Paris and, street by street, reclaimed the city with indiscriminate savagery. As they entered Paris, the city's main buildings and monuments were set on fire by the insurgents. The Tuileries palace and the Hôtel de Ville were burnt down. Hostages were taken and executed on both sides. The Communards arrested the Archbishop of Paris, and then shot him together with a batch of Dominican monks. Resistance finally ended among the graves of the Père-Lachaise cemetery on 28 May when the last combatants were shot in front of the 'Wall of the Confederates'. In that final week of May more people died than in any of the battles during the Franco-Prussian War or in any of the previous massacres in French history (Figure 5). Some 25,000 Parisians, most of them workers, died in the streets at the hands of

5. **Unidentified dead insurgents of the Paris Commune.**

government troops. Over 40,000 Communards were arrested, many were executed, and nearly 5,000 deported to New Caledonia.

Zola re-entered the city before the bloodbath was over and sent eyewitness accounts to *Le Sémaphore*. He described the corpses piled up under the bridges—heads, arms, and legs horribly dislocated, convulsed faces sticking out of the mass of bodies (*Le Sémaphore*, 31 May). He was among the first to venture into the Père-Lachaise cemetery. He was sickened by the campaign of retribution that followed the defeat of the Commune. As the military tribunals and firing squads carried on their work, he cried out for clemency. Neither ordinary citizens, nor even their leaders, were criminals, he argued; the Commune was a symptom of the extreme hardship caused by the long winter of siege and starvation.

The two-month rule of the Commune and its brutal suppression left a permanent mark on French public life. It intensified class hatred and provided French (and European) socialism with an enduring legend. The conservative bourgeoisie constructed a different myth—of Paris as a hotbed of sedition. For them the Commune embodied all their fears of proletarian revolution, and they used it as justification for outright reaction. The city was kept in a state of effective martial law until 1876. There was strict press control. The Second Empire's network of spies and informers was largely maintained. The avowed aim of the Duc de Broglie, the leader of the monarchist majority in the National Assembly who became prime minister in 1873, was to re-establish 'moral order'. His government was strongly religious as well as reactionary. On 24 July 1873 the Assembly voted for the building on the Montmartre hilltop of a basilica, the Sacré-Cœur, 'to expiate the crimes of the Communards'. Zola, uneasy in the stifling atmosphere of surveillance and Moral Order, continued to write for *La Cloche* and *Le Sémaphore de Marseille*. As an outspoken republican, he was himself kept under watch by the police.

Spies

Florent is portrayed as a political fantasist and the 'conspiracy' as a farce. On the other hand, Zola's satirical critique of the bourgeoisie and the 'high' capitalism of the Second Empire in *The Belly of Paris* is unrelenting. The last words of the novel, which belong to Lisa's nephew, the painter Claude Lantier, are: 'Respectable people…What bastards!' Beneath the outward respectability of the bourgeoisie there is a venality that Zola portrays as monstrous.

The brutality of the bourgeoisie is matched by the authoritarianism of the government. One of the most striking features of the novel is its exposé of the regime's machinery of political surveillance. The activity of surveillance assumes global proportions. Images of windows, mirrors, watchful eyes, and attentive ears proliferate. When Florent returns to Paris, he imagines the police watching at every street corner. Almost everyone plays detective: Lisa is concerned to keep an eye on Florent and his activities; Lisa and

Louise Méhudin keep each other under close scrutiny; the trio of gossips—Mademoiselle Saget, La Sarriette, Madame Lecoeur—keep the Quenus and Florent under constant watch; Monsieur Lebigre and other police-agents spy on Florent and the other conspirators in Lebigre's bar.

Mademoiselle Saget's quest to know everything about everyone is a caricatural expression of the system of global surveillance. Her elevated view of Les Halles comes to stand for the government's use of all its subjects to police each other.

> …sitting at her window, she would complete her report. The window was very high up, commanding a view of all the neighbouring houses, and it gave her endless pleasure. At all hours of the day she would install herself there, as though it were an observatory from which she kept watch on everything that went on below her. (p. 237)

Strategically located in the centre of the neighbourhood, the old woman's attic window is emblematic of a collective obsession with panoptic vision. 'Panopticon' was the name given by Jeremy Bentham (the English philosopher, jurist, and social reformer, 1748–1832) to a proposed form of prison built radially so that a guard at a central position could at all times observe the prisoners without being seen himself. The Panopticon provides an extremely apposite model for political control in *The Belly of Paris*. The effect of panopticism is to provoke the fear that there is always someone watching you, and what makes this mode of power all the more effective is the internalization of the practice. Having searched Florent's room, Lisa resolves to denounce him to the police, and she strengthens her resolve by recalling the advice of the local priest. Spying on others, he had implied, is an honourable act, since it is for the public good.

The last stage of Florent's relationship with the people of the market illustrates perfectly both the efficiency of the state's system of surveillance and Florent's role in uniting the community against him. When Lisa arrives at the Palais de Justice, she learns that there already exists a bulging file on him. Virtually all the people of the market have denounced him anonymously; moreover, he has been under surveillance ever since his return to France. As Lisa prepares to leave the police headquarters, making her way through the halls and along the corridors, she feels 'as if she had been caught in the grip of this police world which, she was now sure, saw and knew everything' (p. 244).

The world of food

When we first see Florent, it is as a skeletal figure who has passed out from exhaustion on the road to Paris. Since the events of December 1851, he has been hungry. Back in Paris, he finds it fat and sleek, glutted with food. The novel turns on Florent's consequent malaise. In the opening chapter, the painter Claude takes Florent on a tour of the markets. Claude's aesthetic delight in the myriad still lifes on display (vegetables, meat, fruit, fish, flowers) is juxtaposed with Florent's dysphoric vision of excess. Confronted by a world of unimaginable abundance, Florent is nauseated.

The Quenus' *charcuterie* is the central symbol of the larger symbolic world of the markets. A temple of gluttony, the shop enshrines the values of its owners, who are the very model of the petty bourgeoisie. Lisa, standing behind the counter, is the shop's presiding deity, assimilated into the *charcuterie* as if she were part of its display (Box 3).

Lisa represents the small shopkeepers who support the Empire because they think it is good for business. The ambitious apprentice butcher Auguste, and his betrothed, his cousin Augustine, mirror their employers: Auguste is a pale version of Quenu and Augustine an immature Lisa. Their name-identification reinforces their reflection of the bourgeoisie's political investment in conformity and its own self-reproduction.

Box 3 Lisa and her *charcuterie*

Lisa remained standing at her counter, her head turned slightly in the direction of Les Halles. Florent gazed at her in silence ... In front of her was an array of white china dishes, *saucissons* from Arles and Lyons, slices of which had already been cut off, tongues and pieces of boiled pork, a pig's head in jelly, an open jar of *rillettes*, and a large tin of sardines whose broken lid revealed a pool of oil. On the right and left, on wooden boards, were mounds of French and Italian brawn, a common French ham, of a pinky hue, and a York ham, whose deep red lean stood out beneath a broad band of fat ... Around her rose the smell of all the cooking meats; she was as if enveloped, in her heavy calm, by the aroma of truffles ... The whiteness of all the dishes heightened the whiteness of her apron and sleeves, and set off her plump neck and rosy cheeks, which had the same soft tones as the hams and the same transparent pallor as the fats. As Florent continued to gaze at her he began to feel intimidated, disturbed by the dignity of her carriage; and instead of openly looking at her he glanced furtively in the mirrors around the shop, which reflected her from the back, the front, and the side ... The shop seemed filled with a crowd of Lisas, showing off their broad shoulders, powerful arms, and large breasts so smooth and passionless that they aroused no greater desire than the sight of a belly would ... All down the marble of the walls, and all down the mirrors, sides of pork and strips of larding fat hung from hooks; and Lisa, with her thick neck, rounded hips, and swelling bosom, looked like the queen of all this dangling fat and meat.

(*The Belly of Paris*, chapter 2, pp. 62–3)

Florent's return threatens to disrupt the Quenus' existence. They 'looked at him with the surprise of fat people gripped by a vague feeling of unease at the sight of someone who is thin' (p. 36).

The struggle between the Fat and the Thin, developed through a pattern of hyperbolic contrasts, gives the novel its plot and symbolic structure. When Claude outlines to Florent his concept of the battle between the Fat and the Thin, he takes it right back to Cain and Abel: 'Cain,' he said, 'was a Fat Man and Abel a Thin one. Ever since the first murder, the big eaters have sucked the lifeblood out of the small eaters' (p. 191). The story of Florent is, as Naomi Schor has aptly remarked, 'the story of Cain and Abel as retold by Darwin'. Schor argues persuasively that, in terms of the novel's allegorical structure, Florent functions as a human scapegoat. The story tells how the innocent Florent and the political convictions of 1848 are sacrificed to the new, corrupted order of the Second Empire.

Les Halles, and their agent Lisa, seem to take possession of Florent. He is numbed by the atmosphere of comfort and well-being in the *charcuterie*. Affected by the smell of meat from the counter, he feels himself sinking into a state of torpor. The smell that affects him, however, is not just the smell of the meat, but the smell of order and sanctity exhaled by Lisa and the world she represents. The *charcuterie*, drowned in fat, weakens his will in the face of the relentless pressure Lisa exerts on him to take the job as inspector in the fish market. With the making of black pudding (pp. 78–88), the kitchen assumes a hellish appearance. It drips with grease. Florent's resistance to taking the job slowly melts along with the bacon fat in Quenu's three big pots. He begins work in Les Halles. The *charcuterie* is now happy. Florent is enveloped, however, by the Quenus' bourgeois ideology rather than being the object of their generosity. After eight months in the markets, 'his life had become so calm and regular that he hardly felt he was alive at all' (p. 119). By degrees he becomes sickened once more by the masses of food among which he lives. The rekindling of his interest in politics is marked by one of the novel's global descriptions of Les Halles, in which the markets are seen, through Florent's feverish imagination, as an omnivorous monster (Figure 6). Les Halles, and the nightmare world of food they

6. Les Halles in the 1860s.

represent, are correlated with the Second Empire; and bourgeois devotion to food is equated with devotion to the government:

> Les Halles were the shopkeepers' belly, the belly of respectable petit-bourgeois people, bursting with contentment and well-being, shining in the sun, and declaring that everything was for the best, since respectable people had never before grown so wonderfully fat.
>
> (pp. 124–5)

Food, sex, money

The novel's treatment of sex must be placed within a matrix that equates food, money, and repression. Food and money function as substitutes for sexual desire. The young Lisa and Quenu first meet in the shop of Uncle Gradelle, where they work in the kitchen. Their hands meet over the sausage-meat: 'sometimes she helped him, holding the sausage skins with her plump fingers while he filled them with meat and *lardons*' (p. 46). Their courtship, such as it is, is never explicitly acknowledged. When Gradelle suddenly dies, Lisa discovers his money; she invites Quenu into her bedroom for the first time, pouring the gold and silver coins out on the bed, which is left rumpled as if after an act of love. After counting the money together, they come downstairs as, already, man and wife.

> She and her husband carried on living as before, as the very best of friends and in perfect harmony. She still met him in the shop, their hands still met over the sausage-meat, she still looked over his shoulder to see what was happening in his pans, and it was still only the big fire in the kitchen that brought a flush to their cheeks.
>
> (p. 49)

In contrast to the Quenus are the young Marjolin and Cadine. Marjolin, as a child, lives like a squirrel in Les Halles, while Cadine, a flower-seller, is a kind of market sprite. Together they create an innocently sexualized idyll, as if personifying the vitality—the Life Force—of the markets. Lisa and the world she represents threaten, and indeed damage, their idyll. In her sleekness and roundness she fascinates Marjolin and, with her genteel caresses, arouses his lust. When she descends into the secret depths of the markets, led by Marjolin through the cellars where live birds are kept in cages, the world of animal sexuality could not be more strongly evoked. It is indeed as an animal that Marjolin is treated when he tries to assault Lisa. She fells him like a stockyard butcher. He collapses, smashing his head against the edge of a stone block. She steals away, untroubled, leaving him a semi-idiot. Afterwards, she briefly continues to enjoy, now with impunity, her caresses of Marjolin's chin; but she soon desists: 'It was a small pleasure she had allowed herself, and now regretted' (p. 183). Her sexuality remains repressed, buried under her massive 'respectability', her body forever enclosed in her huge white apron.

A similar sublimation of sexuality is evident in Florent. From the moment he returns to Les Halles, he is disturbed not only by masses of food but also by masses of female flesh. The female stallholders in the fish market are beautiful, but he feels no desire for them. At the height of his persecution by the fishwives, he seems pursued by swirling skirts, monstrous hips, and huge breasts. The breasts of one, La Normande, exude a pungent mixture of fishy smells that mingle with the general stench of the markets. As the novel progresses, Florent comes to see in Les Halles a place of death, 'a charnel house reeking with foul smells and putrefaction' (p. 189). It is from this dead, foul-smelling world that he seeks to escape through his political fantasies.

Description

The originality of *The Belly of Paris* has nothing to do with its plot. The plot is slight, and in any case the reader of 1873 knew that there was no popular uprising in Paris in 1858. The novel's originality lies, rather, in Zola's stylistic experiment with description; in his desire to test the limits of descriptive discourse. His descriptions are remarkably luxuriant, with their methodically developed lists, their compendia of names and terms, their lexical borrowings from art criticism, and their elaborate synaesthetic effects (the celebrated 'cheese symphony' is but one of several bravura pieces). Zola is famous for his descriptions, but in no other novel of his are they so abundant. *The Belly of Paris* is nothing if not a novel of spectacle. Claude and Cadine are *flâneurs* who circulate constantly in and around Les Halles, eagerly soaking up the sights of the markets and the neighbouring streets (see Box 4). The novel unfolds like a series of enormous still lifes or brilliant tableaux reminiscent of Pieter Bruegel (*c.*1525–1569) or Hieronymus Bosch (*c.*1450–1516).

Zola's preparatory work for the novel inaugurated the 'naturalist' method he used systematically in his subsequent novels. For several weeks in May and June of 1872, he explored Les Halles in all its aspects, at all hours of day and night, and in all kinds of light and weather conditions. He also explored the adjoining streets—narrow, cobbled, often insalubrious, the 'old Paris' that

Box 4 The *flâneur*

The *flâneur* is a literary and artistic figure born in 19th-century Paris. The French noun *flâneur* means 'stroller', 'idler', or 'loiterer'. *Flânerie* is the act of strolling, with all of its accompanying associations. The *flâneur* is a street idler, a person who loiters, a kind of artist of impressions, wandering aimlessly and anonymously through the city, giving himself (or herself) over to the spectacle of the moment. He (or she) is an urban explorer, a connoisseur of the street, with its endlessly varied and changing sights. The German philosopher and cultural critic Walter Benjamin (1892–1940), drawing on the poetry of Charles Baudelaire, made the *flâneur* an object of scholarly interest in the 20th century, as an emblem of modern urban experience. Following Benjamin, the *flâneur* has become an important symbol for scholars, artists, and writers. Recent scholarship has also proposed the *flâneuse*, a female equivalent to the *flâneur*.

had escaped demolition under Haussmann. He took exhaustive notes on his impressions of the teeming life of the markets: the fantastic shapes of the iron and glass structures; the myriad types of food; the various vendors and tradespeople; the colourful types (the market-porters with their wide-brimmed hats, the road-sweepers with their big brooms, the sellers of rat-poison, etc.). He even arranged for a security guard to show him round the cellars under the markets and to take him on a tour of the roofs. This on-the-spot observation was complemented by research in secondary sources (books about the market's history and system of organization) and by interviews with tradespeople and workers. This preparatory material infuses the text of *The Belly of Paris*, giving it a richly documentary quality.

The power of the novel (as of Zola's novels generally) does not come, however, from its documentary richness, nor from the detail of its descriptions, but from its imaginative qualities. It is literature, not a document; it is fiction, not an inventory. The hallmarks of Zola's fiction are its movement, colour, and atmospheric intensity. Zola shows the interaction of man and milieu not as a concept but in dramatic and vivid images, making the themes palpable, visible, smellable.

Zola's fiction is especially remarkable for its symbolizing effects. *The Belly of Paris* is the first of his novels to be built round a great central image. Les Halles, a giant figuration of bourgeois consumer society, play as important a part in the narrative as any of the characters. The markets swallow Florent, like the whale swallowing Jonah, and spew him out eventually like a piece of waste matter. His expulsion brings back peace, harmony, and above all, health: 'Once again the *charcuterie* exuded health, a kind of greasy health' (p. 275). The sausages have regained their lustre, order has been restored, the belly is triumphant.

Chapter 4
'A work of truth':
L'Assommoir

Zola's assault on the forces of 'respectability' reached an early peak in 1877, when he published his first great novel of working-class life, *L'Assommoir* (Box 5). As Philip Walker has commented in his critical biography of Zola, in France in the 1870s there was no more original, timely, or audacious fictional topic to be found. The modern French industrial proletariat was being born. Since the last years of the Empire there had been a number of major strikes, all brutally suppressed. The workers were organizing into unions, the international revolutionary movement had been gaining momentum, and the trauma of the Commune of 1871 was still fresh in people's minds. Haussmann's remaking of Paris, involving massive slum clearance, had forced the workers out of the centre of the city into the suburbs, creating what was in effect two distinct cities: the Paris of Luxury and the Paris of Poverty. 'The Parisian bourgeoisie eyed this new community encircling their own with a mixture of curiosity, contempt, guilt, and fear.'

'Filth'

The novel was a publishing sensation: 100,000 copies were sold by 1881. The fascination of *L'Assommoir* was due in large measure to the novelty, and contemporaneity, of its subject matter. It was also scandalous. The serialization in *Le Bien public* from April 1876 had come to an abrupt halt because of protests from provincial

Box 5 *L'Assommoir*: a summary

Set in a slum area in Paris behind the Gare du Nord, *L'Assommoir* focuses on the life and death of a washerwoman, Gervaise Macquart, the second daughter of Antoine Macquart. It describes the tragic unravelling of her modest hopes of happiness in the face of a hostile environment and a hereditary predisposition to drink. Abandoned by her shiftless lover Lantier, the father of her two children, Étienne and Claude, she marries a roofer, Coupeau. Though easygoing, she is hard-working and virtuous, and for a while their household prospers. A daughter, Anna (later nicknamed Nana), is born. Coupeau has an accident that leaves him a cripple; he becomes idle and turns to drink. However, Gervaise sets up her own laundry business with the help of a loan from an admirer, Goujet. But when Lantier returns and moves in with her and Coupeau, forming a *ménage à trois*, her life degenerates. She descends into drink and poverty. Reduced to a life of squalor, she starves to death in a niche under a tenement stairway.

subscribers about the novel's purported indecency and the crudity of its language; the newspaper, which was radically republican, also felt that the novel's political standpoint was unclear. The serialization was picked up and continued by a weekly literary review, *La République des lettres*. Meanwhile, a number of bourgeois critics, confronted by the novel's unflinchingly graphic descriptions of urban squalor, noisily accused Zola of pornography. In *Le Figaro* on 1 September 1876, Albert Millaud wrote: 'This is not realism, it is filth; it is not vulgarity, it is pornography.' In *Le Journal des débats* on 14 March 1877, Henri Houssaye wrote: '*L'Assommoir*…belongs less to literature than to pathology.' The hostile reactions to *L'Assommoir*, together with its immense popular success, indicated that something significantly new had happened to the novel. Zola was attacked by both right

Box 6 The first novel about the common people that does not lie

When *L'Assommoir* was serialized in a newspaper, it was attacked with unprecedented ferocity, denounced, and charged with all manner of crimes. Do I really need to explain here, in these few lines, what my authorial intentions were? I wanted to depict the inexorable downfall of a working-class family in the poisonous atmosphere of our city slums. Alcoholism and idleness lead to a weakening of family ties, to the filth of promiscuity, to the progressive loss of decent feelings, and ultimately to degradation and death. It is simply morality in action.

L'Assommoir is without doubt the most moral of my books. I have often had occasion to write about far more horrifying social sores. It is the novel's form that has shocked people. People have taken exception to the words. My crime is to have had the literary curiosity to gather together the language of the common people and present it in a carefully fashioned mould. Yes indeed, the novel's form—there lies my great crime! ...

In any case I am not defending myself. My novel will be my defence. It is a work of truth, the first novel about the common people that does not lie and that has the authentic smell of the people. And readers should not conclude that the people as a whole are bad, for my characters are not bad, but only ignorant and brought low by the conditions of sweated toil and poverty in which they live. All I ask is that my novels be read, understood, and seen clearly in their context, before they are subjected to the ready-made, grotesque, and odious judgments that are circulating about me and my works. If only people knew ... that the fearsome, bloodthirsty novelist is in fact a respectable bourgeois, devoted to learning and art, living in quiet seclusion ...

(Zola, Preface to *L'Assommoir*, 1 January 1877)

and left. The left accused him of depicting the workers in a grossly negative light, and objected to the absence of any overt political commentary; while conservative critics clearly considered that he had transgressed the limits of what could be written about. To focus entirely on industrial workers was new and disturbing, and to make a working-class washerwoman a tragic heroine even more so. If the workers could take over the novel, perhaps, as the Commune had appeared so alarmingly to foretell, they could also take over the government. The attacks on *L'Assommoir* for pornography were motivated as much by reactionary fear as by prudishness.

When the novel appeared in book form, Zola added a preface in response to the storm of controversy it had aroused. The moral and political implications of his novel, he argued, were implicit. And far from misrepresenting the workers, he was the first novelist to represent the workers as they really were (Box 6).

Description and empathy

The 'truth' of the novel is embodied partly in descriptions characterized by their immense realistic detail: their hyper-realism. These descriptions evoke, in vividly precise terms, the everyday living and working conditions of Zola's characters. Here is an extract from the description, in the opening chapter, of the washhouse where Gervaise works:

> Everywhere there was a clinging dampness, like fine rain, heavy with the smell of soap, a stale, dank, persistent smell sharpened at times by a whiff of bleach. Standing at the wash-boards along each side of the central aisle were rows of women, their sleeves rolled right up to their shoulders, their necks bare, their skirts hitched up, showing their coloured stockings and heavy laced boots. They were beating away like mad, laughing, leaning back to yell something above the din, then bending forward again over their tubs, a foul-mouthed, rough, ungainly lot, soaked through as if they had

been caught in a downpour, their skin red and steaming. All round and under them water was slopping about, hot water from buckets carried over and tipped out in one go, cold water from taps left on and pissing away, splashes from beaters, drips from washing already rinsed, and the puddles they were standing in trickling away in rivulets over the uneven stone floor. And, amid the shouting, the rhythmic thumping, the soft patter of rain—this storm of noise muffled by the wet ceiling—the boiler, over to the right, covered with a fine dew, completely white, panted and snorted continuously, as if the frenzied vibration of its fly-wheel was regulating the whole monstrous uproar.

A defining feature of Zola's originality is the phenomenological quality of his writing: the sensory immediacy that informs his characters' relationship with their physical environment, which, together with the accumulation of authentic detail, leads the reader to empathize with them, to see and *feel* the world as they do.

Empathy, in the sense of being able to understand and share the feelings of a character, is reflected in Zola's use of point of view. His various narrative worlds, with their specific atmospheres, are always presented through the eyes of individuals, and are never separate from human experience. Often, the first chapter recounts the arrival of a stranger in a community: Florent in *The Belly of Paris*, suddenly appearing in the midst of the people of Les Halles; Étienne Lantier in *Germinal*, arriving in the mining village, being introduced to the life of the *coron*, and descending into the mine for the first time; Denise Baudu in *The Ladies' Paradise*, arriving in Paris and coming, open-mouthed, upon the new department store; and Gervaise in *L'Assommoir*, recently arrived in the city from Plassans, surveying the street from her hotel window, and later (in the second chapter) accompanying Coupeau when he visits the slum tenement where his sister and brother-in-law live and where Gervaise herself will come to live and, eventually, die. She waits outside, and gazes at the house.

Gervaise looked up and studied the front of the building. On the street side it had five floors, each with fifteen windows in a line, the black shutters of which, with their broken slats, gave the vast expanse of wall a look of utter desolation. Below, on the ground floor, there were four shops: to the right of the doorway a huge, greasy eating-house, to the left a coal merchant's, a draper's and an umbrella shop. The building looked all the more colossal because it was situated between two rickety little shacks, pressed against it on either side; square-shaped, like a roughly cast block of cement, crumbling and flaking in the rain, this enormous, crude cube stood out against the pale sky, high above the surrounding rooftops, its mud-coloured sides, unplastered and as stark and interminable as prison walls, showing rows of toothing-stones, like decaying jaws gaping in the void.

She ventures into the courtyard and notices the 'filth', the 'miserable poverty', and the 'grime'. She looks up again, and is 'astonished at the sheer size of the place, feeling she was in the middle of some living organism, in the very heart of a city, fascinated by the building as if she were in the presence of some gigantic human being'. During a subsequent visit, as she prepares to leave, it seems to her 'that the house was on top of her, crushing her under its weight, icy on her shoulders'. Both immensely detailed and metaphorically charged, the description of the tenement house extends intermittently over a dozen pages. It is a part of the documentation that grounds the novel in social reality, and a poetic symbol of the fears and apprehensions of Gervaise and the baleful forces that do eventually crush her.

Narrative innovation

The effect of empathy is heightened by Zola's innovative narrative technique. He makes brilliant use of the free indirect style (*style indirect libre*) pioneered by Gustave Flaubert (and, in English literature, by Jane Austen) to express a character's thoughts and feelings without any explanatory 'he/she said/thought'. Zola's narrative voice, instead of keeping at a distance from the language of the workers, often adopts that language, blurring the lines between the characters and the narrator. Instead of encountering the workers through the cultured and aloof voice of a bourgeois narrator, which contemporary readers would have been expecting, they encounter the workers themselves. It is as if the working-class characters take on a narrative function, telling their own story. The reader is thus brought into more direct and authentic contact with them and their world than would have been the case with more conventional narrative. As Zola indicated in his preface, this is what disturbed his bourgeois critics most: 'It is the novel's form that has shocked people. People have taken exception to the words.' The workers are intrusively present—they can be 'smelt'—in the very language of *L'Assommoir*.

Zola's concern to reproduce working-class speech forms led him, in his preparatory work for the novel, to compile a lexicon on the basis mainly of Alfred Delvau's dictionary of urban slang, *Dictionnaire de la langue verte* (1866), and Denis Poulot's vivid documentary of the Parisian worker, *La Question sociale: le sublime ou le travailleur comme il est en 1870 et ce qu'il peut être* (1870)—though it is important to note that these served as supplements to the first-hand knowledge he gained while living in the impoverished parts of Paris between 1858 and 1862.

The novel's central chapter (chapter 7) describes Gervaise's celebration of her saint's day with a Rabelaisian feast where all the main characters are gathered together and food, drink, and companionship are the focus. The doors and windows are opened and the whole neighbourhood is invited to join in the merrymaking. The feast is a pivotal episode, marking the high point of Gervaise's professional success, but also a turning-point in her fortunes. The sheer extravagance of the meal suggests the lurking dangers of dissipation, and the occasion also marks the fateful return of Lantier, Gervaise's malevolent former lover.

Above all, the extravagance expresses defiance, through recklessness and prodigality, of the constrictions—the prudence and thrift—of a life always on the brink of starvation. The workers' plight is expressed through the very description of their pleasure: 'The whole shop was dying for a binge. They needed an absolute blow-out.' The meal becomes an orgy, and the mounting excitement of the characters is matched by that of the narrative voice, which appears to blend joyously with the voices of the assembled company:

> God, yes, they really stuffed themselves! If you're going to do it, you might as well do it properly, eh? And if you only have a real binge once in a blue moon, you'd be bloody mad not to fill yourself up to the eyeballs. You could actually see their bellies getting bigger by the minute! The women looked as if they were pregnant. Every one of 'em fit to burst, the greedy pigs! Their mouths wide-open, grease all over their chins, their faces were just like backsides, and so red you'd swear they were rich people's backsides, with money pouring out of them.
>
> And the wine, my friends! The wine flowed round the table like the water flowing in the Seine.

The past definite tense used in the first sentence ('on s'en flanqua une bosse!'/'they really stuffed themselves') clearly identifies the passage as a part of the narrative, but the register and syntax—direct, simple, robustly colloquial—reflect the language of the characters. The characters' colloquial language is woven into the fabric of the narrative, absorbing the written discourse of the narrator. The use of *on* in the original ('et si l'on...') is ambiguous ('as if [they? we?]...'), blurring further the distinction between narrator and characters. A single voice dominates. The jovial apostrophe 'my friends!', its author and addressees uncertain, draws the reader into sharing in the general euphoria. The narrator sits at the table with his characters, participating stylistically in the revelry and implicitly inviting the reader to join in too, thus subverting the moralistic perspectives on the workers' intemperance that so strongly marked contemporary discourse on social issues and contemporary reactions to the novel. Is it because Gervaise is self-indulgent and given to excess that she undergoes the tragedy of working people? Or is it because she undergoes the tragedy of working people that she becomes self-indulgent and given to excess? Zola showed his bourgeois readers things they would prefer not to see in a style making it impossible to look the other way (Figure 7).

Description and metaphor

The aim of the naturalist novel was to set human beings in their environment and to explain its effects on them. Description, by evoking the interaction between people and their environments, necessarily has a privileged place in Zola's work. As he wrote in an article entitled 'On Description' ('De la description'): 'We consider that man cannot be separated from his milieu...This explains what people call our interminable descriptions.' The Hungarian Marxist critic György Lukács famously condemned naturalism as mere reportage. But documentary detail, though it helps to create ethnographically rich evocations of particular milieux, is not an end in itself. The observed reality of the world is the foundation for a poetic vision, though it is a vision rooted in a specific, there-and-then reality. Zola blends the everyday and the fantastic. What makes his writing so compelling is its metaphoric dimensions: its sur-realism.

Early in *L'Assommoir* (chapter 2), Gervaise is invited to a neighbourhood bar, with its clientele of alcoholics, and there she gazes at the distilling machine at the back of the bar. She is curious about it, but is immediately aware of its sinister qualities. It seems alive and malevolent, crouching in the courtyard like some monstrous animal:

> The still, with its strangely-shaped containers and its endless coils of piping, had a forbidding look; there was no steam coming out of

7. Edgar Degas, *In a Café* (also called *Absinthe*), 1876–7. Some of the most subtly disquieting images of urban modernity are embodied in the paintings of Edgar Degas. An outstanding example is *In a Café*. The focal point of this painting is the face of the woman, with her vacant, stupefied look: a brilliant image of disconnection. The woman is entirely cut off from the man next to her, who is gazing out of the picture. The painting (first exhibited in 1876, the year in which Zola published *L'Assommoir* in serial form) could be used as an illustration for Zola's description in Chapter 10 of his novel of Gervaise getting drunk on absinthe in the bar, 'The Assommoir', frequented by her husband and his mates.

it, but you could just hear a kind of breathing inside it, like a subterranean rumbling…

Much later (chapter 10), when alcohol has begun to destroy her life, her curiosity becomes a kind of hypnotism, and the still's malevolence assumes the quality of nightmare:

> She turned round and saw the still, the booze-machine, working away in the little glassed-in yard, its devil's kitchen rumbling away deep inside it. At night the copper containers looked duller, lit just by red, star-shaped reflections on their curved surfaces; and the shadow cast by the machine on the wall behind it conjured up obscene shapes, figures with tails, monsters opening their jaws as if to swallow them all up.

The idea of the machine as a monster is adumbrated in the earlier references to the boiler in the washhouse, with its ceaseless vibrating and snorting; and it is continued when Gervaise visits a bolt and rivet factory (chapter 6) with her friend, the metalworker Goujet:

> The huge shed was shaking with the vibration of the machines; great shadows floated about, streaked fiery red,…[S]he followed him, into a deafening din made up of all kinds of hissing and rumbling noises, among clouds of smoke peopled with weird shapes, black figures rushing about, machines waving their arms, she couldn't make out which was which.

Gervaise's sense of disorientation, and her deep unease, are symbolic of the feelings of many in the face of growing industrialization. Goujet shows Gervaise how he makes rivets out of white-hot metal, gently tapping out 300 20-millimetre rivets a day with his five-pound hammer. But that craft is under threat, for the boss is installing some new machinery which can produce rivets in greater quantity and more efficiently than any worker:

The steam-engine was in a corner, behind a low brick wall...In twelve hours this blasted contraption turned out hundreds of kilos of them. Goujet was not a vindictive man, but there were times when he would gladly...have smashed up all this metal, in sheer anger at the fact that its arms were stronger than his. It upset him, even though he told himself that human flesh couldn't fight against iron. The day would come, of course, when the machines would kill off the manual worker; already their daily wage had dropped from twelve francs to nine, and there was talk of more cuts to come.

Tragic vision

Environment and heredity pursue Gervaise as relentlessly as the forces of Fate in an ancient tragedy. As Valerie Minogue has shown in her excellent study of *L'Assommoir*, the pathos of the workers' experience is heightened by allusions to a lost Eden of innocence and happiness, as well as by the workers' pride in their work and skills, and their unconscious hankering after a perfection of craftsmanship doomed in the dawning era of soulless mass production. The novel is threaded with images and metaphors that, however fleetingly, carry the everyday and often sordid reality to a more heroic and mythic level: the story of humanity born to majesty, but fallen and degraded. In this reading, the sense of 'human dignity betrayed and brought low' emerges as the essential theme of *L'Assommoir*.

The novel is a masterpiece of design (symmetries, echoes, contrasts, patterns of repetition), descriptive and symbolic power, atmospheric and sensuous intensity, and narrative technique. Henry James, in a long essay on Zola in *The Atlantic Monthly* of August 1903, wrote: '[Gervaise's] career, as presented, has...the largeness that, throughout the chronicle, we feel as epic, and the intensity of her creator's vision of it and of the dense sordid life hanging about it one of the great things the modern novel has been able to do.' *L'Assommoir* made Zola famous. It established his reputation as the most important writer of his generation; and ironically, given its subject matter, it made him rich. It turned him, materially speaking, into a bourgeois.

Zola's financial situation had been improving steadily throughout the 1870s. In 1874 he had moved with his wife and mother to a three-storey house with a garden in the Rue Saint-Georges (now Rue des Apennins). They had also been able to take long summer holidays by the sea, at Saint-Aubin in Normandy, in 1876, and at Piriac in Brittany, the following year. But with the newly acquired wealth accruing from his *L'Assommoir* royalties, he moved the household again, in April 1877, this time to a well-appointed apartment in the Rue de Boulogne (now Rue Ballu). Then, in May 1878, he bought a little house at Médan in the Seine valley, about 25 miles from Paris. Almost immediately he started extending and transforming the little house, and never stopped. The little house became a large, oddly shaped villa, containing a great study fifteen feet high, with a huge oak writing table and an enormous Renaissance fireplace inscribed with the gold letters: *Nulla dies sine linea*.

The additions to the property included a guest cottage. Zola began to entertain regularly. Flaubert, Charpentier, Edmond de Goncourt, and Alphonse Daudet were always welcome, as were Zola's so-called disciples: Paul Alexis, Henry Céard, Joris-Karl Huysmans, Léon Hennique, and Guy de Maupassant (the latter having been introduced to Zola by Flaubert). On 16 April 1877, at the Restaurant Trapp, these younger writers, together with Octave Mirbeau, had organized a dinner which was widely seen as the official launch of the naturalist movement. Meanwhile, Zola worked unremittingly to promote naturalism, writing a stream of critical essays in *Vestnik Evropy*, *Le Voltaire*, and *Le Bien public*, and urging his followers to produce naturalist works that would further the cause.

Partly to get the others known, partly to generate publicity, and partly to demonstrate the unity of what had become known as 'the Médan group', he suggested they should collaborate on a volume of short stories which would all deal with the same subject—the Franco-Prussian War. He himself had a story ready: *The Attack on the Mill* (*L'Attaque du moulin*), which had already been published in Russian translation in *Vestnik Evropy*. The others rose to the challenge. The result was *Les Soirées de Médan* (*Evenings at Médan*), which was published by Charpentier in April 1880. The aim of the collection, which contained a story by each writer, was to promote the ideals of naturalism by treating episodes in the Franco-Prussian War in a realistic, ironic, and often unheroic way, in contrast to the patriotic views of the war that were officially promoted after 1870. By far the most famous story in the collection is 'Boule de suif', which immediately launched Maupassant on his distinguished career as a short-story writer.

Naturalist writers, Zola had declared in *Lettre à la jeunesse* ('A Letter to the Young Men of France'), a long essay published in *Le Voltaire* in May 1879, 'want France to be well informed, purged of lyric nonsense, greater for having embraced the culture of truth, confident that the experimental method should be applied to every human endeavour—to politics as to literature, to social economy as to the art of war.'

Chapter 5
The man-eater: *Nana*

Nana, the ninth volume in the Rougon-Macquart series, consists of a number of episodes, or tableaux, in the short but spectacular life of Anna Coupeau, the fourth child of Gervaise Macquart. In *L'Assommoir* we see her working as a florist and dabbling in casual street prostitution. She has a child by an unknown father when she is 16. Having escaped from the slums, in *Nana* she makes her mark first in the theatre, then enters the world of high prostitution, becoming the most celebrated courtesan in Second Empire Paris, wreaking havoc among the upper classes with her rampant sexuality (Figure 8).

The novel opens with a night at the Théâtre des Variétés in April 1867, just after the inauguration of the World Fair (the Exposition Universelle) in Paris. Nana is 18. Zola describes in detail the performance of *La Blonde Vénus*, a fictional operetta modelled after *La Belle Hélène* by Jacques Offenbach (1819–80), in which Nana is cast as the lead. She is the talk of Paris, though this is her first stage appearance. When asked to say something about her talents, Bordenave, the theatre manager, explains that a star does not need to know how to sing or act: 'Nana has something else, for heaven's sake, and something that makes all the other stuff superfluous' (p. 6). At first the audience laughs, thinking her performance terrible, until a youth, Georges Hugon, cries out, 'Amazing.' From then until the end of the play, Nana is in control

LES ROUGON-MACQUART

HISTOIRE NATURELLE ET SOCIALE D'UNE FAMILLE SOUS LE SECOND EMPIRE

NANA

PAR

ÉMILE ZOLA

PARIS

G. CHARPENTIER, ÉDITEUR

13, RUE DE GRENELLE-SAINT-GERMAIN, 13

1880

8. Émile Zola, *Nana* (first edition), 1880.

of the audience, especially in the third act when she appears on stage virtually naked, in the flimsiest of veils, rousing the spectators to a frenzy.

> No one was laughing any more, men's intent faces were straining forward, their noses thin, mouths quickened and dry. It was as though a puff of wind, very gentle but charged with a dull sense of foreboding, had passed over. Suddenly the woman was emerging from the child, causing unease, bringing that madness of their sex, opening up unknown desire. Nana was still smiling but it was the knowing smile of the man-eater.   (p. 24)

In the course of the novel Nana destroys all the men—aristocrats, high government officials, army officers, bankers, journalists—who pursue her, leaving a trail of bankruptcy, humiliation, and death. Symbol of profligacy and excess, she feeds insatiably on her lovers while remaining serenely indifferent to them. Her most notable victim is Comte Muffat de Beuville, Chamberlain to the Empress, an ageing and extremely devout aristocrat, whom she subjugates completely, forcing him to undergo every kind of indignity. In a famous scene, she makes him wear his Court uniform, then take it off and trample and spit on it.

Nana becomes a celebrity:

> Her photographs were displayed in shop windows and she was mentioned in magazines. Heads turned as she went by in her carriage on the boulevard and everyone murmured her name, with admiration, as though doing homage to a sovereign...And the wonder was that this buxom girl, so awkward on stage, so comical as soon as she tried to play a respectable woman, was bewitchingly alluring off stage, without any effort on her part. She...was the aristocrat of vice, splendid, rebellious, walking all over Paris society like an omnipotent mistress. She set the tone and noble ladies copied her.   (p. 244)

While Nana becomes 'a fashionable lady', Muffat's wife, Comtesse Sabine, a pillar of respectable society until her husband has an affair with Nana, becomes addicted to a life of sexual promiscuity. The working-class courtesan and the upper-class woman grow progressively less and less distinguishable.

Nana suddenly disappears, her belongings are auctioned, and no one knows where she is. But even her absence generates all kinds of rumours: 'When her name was mentioned amongst the ladies and gentlemen of her acquaintance, the strangest stories circulated, everybody gave conflicting and fantastic information...A legend was being created...' (p. 363). She has left her sickly infant son in the care of an aunt near Paris, but when a smallpox epidemic breaks out she returns to nurse him; he dies, and she contracts the disease herself. Zola has Nana die a horrible death, in a room at the Grand Hôtel, her smallpox (a euphemism for syphilis) the outward form of the social disease she represents.

Nana is intended to reflect Second Empire society itself—a society given over to the pursuit of pleasure, built on its urges and appetites. Her ravaged body thus comes to symbolize the disfigurement of the social body as a whole. The allegorization of Nana's life and death is clear: she was born in 1852, the year of Louis-Napoleon's coup d'état; the novel opens in the year of the great Exposition Universelle, with the Empire at its most self-congratulatory and carnivalesque; and she dies on the very day that war with Prussia is declared, a prelude to the Empire's collapse. A jingoistic crowd is passing along the boulevard below, but the atmosphere is heavy with a sense of foreboding. The narrative looks forward to the debacle of military defeat, the fall of the Empire, and the bloodshed of the Commune. An ironic rewriting of the opening chapter, the last chapter gathers together all the characters (at least those who have survived) who witnessed Nana's triumphant appearance in *La Blonde Vénus*.

In the final scene, however, the men turn away from her, afraid of being contaminated. Her hideous corpse is left alone in the empty hotel room.

> Venus was decomposing. It was as if the virus she had caught from the gutter, from the carcasses left by the roadside, this ferment with which she had poisoned a whole race, had now come to the surface of her face and rotted it.   (p. 376)

Prostitutes

Zola plays to remarkable effect in *Nana* on male fear (including, it might be said, his own) of the 'natural' woman, and in particular fear that prostitutes might transgress established social boundaries and infiltrate the bourgeoisie and upper class. The novel illustrates, ultimately in apocalyptic vein, how, in the 19th-century social imaginary, the prostitute, whether a common streetwalker or a successful courtesan, became a threatening figure associated with disorder and the overturning of the naturalized hierarchies and institutions of society. For the men of the bourgeoisie and aristocracy, she represents their nightmares—the destruction of moral decorum, family life, patriarchal power, the social order itself. Maxime Du Camp, in his six-volume book on daily life in Paris, *Paris: ses organes, ses fonctions et sa vie jusqu'en 1870* (1869–75), attributed many of the ills of contemporary society to prostitution, characterizing it as a disease, a gangrene arising from the lower depths of society and invading the entire social organism. This vision of prostitution as a source of contamination is evoked in *Nana* in the article written by Fauchery the journalist, in which Nana is compared to a disease-carrying fly:

> She had grown up in the gutter, in the back streets of Paris. A tall, beautiful girl, with superb skin like a plant growing in a dung-heap, she was avenging the wretched and the destitute from whom she

had sprung. In Nana, the immorality that was being allowed to pollute the common people was rising to the surface and rotting the aristocracy. She was becoming a force of nature, an unwitting ferment of destruction, corrupting and throwing the structures of Paris society into disarray between her snowy-white thighs, churning it up, as women each month turn the milk sour. And it was at the end of the article that the comparison with the fly was made; a fly the colour of sunshine, escaped from the midden, a fly which sucks death from the carrion you are wont to see along the roads and which, buzzing and dancing, throwing out a dazzle of jewels, poisons men simply by flying in through the windows of palaces and landing on them.   (p. 170)

At the apex of the great prostitution pyramid was a kind of elite: the courtesans. Nana is a composite figure based on several of these celebrated women, whose lives were built less on sex than on ostentation. They were glamorous status symbols for their male lovers, who flaunted their money by lavishing vast amounts on them. The expense of the courtesan became intrinsic to her allure, and the more money she had, the more she spent; extravagance became almost a professional duty. Thérèse Lachmann, a notorious Polish-born Jewish courtesan known as La Païva, had an opulent *hôtel particulier* built for her on the Champs-Élysées, where it stands today, a listed building, home of the Travellers' Club, and a monument to the lifestyle of the Second Empire courtesan.

Napoleon III's Second Empire was the golden age of the courtesan, for she embodied Imperial society's delight in conspicuous consumption, its taste for show, its culture of leisure and pleasure. The courtesan symbolized the regime itself. This is suggested by the connotations of the term coined for the courtesan's world: *demi-monde*, that is, a shadowy half-world in which nothing is quite what it seems and the image is frequently taken for the reality. The Second Empire always lived under the shadow of illegitimacy, for it originated in a coup d'état; and Virginia

Rounding has written perceptively of Napoleon III's desire to draw a form of legitimacy from his illustrious uncle Napoleon I:

> [The] imperial court could be seen as mirroring and sharing some of the essence of the *demi-monde*, not only in its ostentation but also in its shadowiness, its sense of unreality and its flair for imitation, and the women, like La Païva, who rose to startling prominence through an accumulation of wealth about whose origins it was best not to enquire too closely shared some of the characteristics of the Emperor who had arisen out of a lifetime of exile and relative anonymity to claim what he considered to be the inheritance of his uncle…

The *demi-monde* formed a kind of parallel world existing alongside the *haut monde*. The most illustrious courtesans became quasi-celebrities, enjoying prominent positions in society. During the 1850s, for example, Apollonie Sabatier kept a political and literary salon at her house in the Rue Frochot. It was frequented by the eminent writers Gustave Flaubert and Charles Baudelaire. The latter even dedicated some of the poems in *Les Fleurs du mal* (*The Flowers of Evil*) to her. 'The *demi-monde* knew how to copy the *haut monde* and yet at the same time the *haut monde* was not above copying the half-world, particularly where fashionable dress was concerned.'

While men were able to move relatively easily between the two worlds, they felt that 'virtuous' women—middle-class wives, mothers, and daughters—needed protection, lest they be corrupted. It was this fear of corruption that caused such disquiet among contemporary writers such as Maxime Du Camp when describing the difficulty of knowing whether respectable women were dressing like prostitutes, or prostitutes were dressing like respectable women. And it was this fear that lay behind the male pathologization of women and the female body—the splitting of women into 'housewife or harlot'—throughout the 19th century.

Theatre

The physical decor of the theatre has rich metaphoric connotations. The description of the auditorium in the opening chapter reflects Zola's view of the tawdriness of the Second Empire: the huge crystal chandelier and the heavy crimson curtain, 'rich as those of some fabulous palace, were in stark contrast to the shabby surrounds, where large cracks were visible beneath the gilt' (p. 9). In chapter 5 Muffat's journey backstage with the Prince of Scotland, through the noises and smells of the theatre—the mingled scents of grease-paint, sweat, women's perfume, and the 'dubious undergarments' (p. 109) of the female extras—inflames his erotic imagination. His long, unnerving walk through the wings, in which he gets lost, is a journey into his unconscious, prefiguring his entrapment in the labyrinth that is Nana. His backstage visit becomes a descent into the underworld. Almost unable to breathe, he is overcome by the dank, murky environment of the woman's sex: 'It was like a subterranean existence down there in the dark depths, men's voices sounding as if they were ascending from a cave' (p. 109). After watching Nana naked on stage through a peep-hole in the back of the set, he climbs the stairs to her dressing-room: 'For a moment he had to catch hold of the iron balustrade that was warm to his touch, it seemed warm with life, he closed his eyes and with one breath filled his lungs with the whole sexuality of woman, as yet unknown, but which was now coming at him full in the face' (p. 125).

Even the non-theatrical spaces in the novel resemble the world of the stage. A case in point, as Ilona Chessid has noted, is the palatial town house Muffat buys for Nana in the Avenue de Villiers. Zola describes the delegation of various functions to specific areas of the house. A staircase in the kitchen, for example, leads to the street and therefore permits discreet exits and entrances. As Chessid puts it, Nana's chambermaid, Zoé, 'acts as stage manager of the elaborate production that is Nana's personal life'.

Zoé arranged everything, sorted out even the most unforeseen complications. It was like a well-oiled machine, a theatre, regulated like a huge business enterprise, and functioned with such precision that for the first months there were no hitches or disasters.

(pp. 248–9)

Later, when Nana's life begins to run out of control, the 'production' takes on some of the qualities of farce. The house becomes 'a theatre run amok'. Doors open and close, with men constantly coming and going, often having to be hidden by Zoé, who spends most of her time ushering in and concealing untimely clients.

'Theatre', as David Baguley has observed, 'is . . . the very essence of the world the novel depicts'. This is true, not only in terms of the theatricality of the Second Empire itself, with its investment in show and self-aggrandizement, but also in terms of the sexual hypocrisy permeating upper-class society. Nana learns through her friend Satin that respectability is an illusion, a simple matter of appearances: 'the most respectable-looking were the most depraved. The whole veneer cracked, the beast appeared, very demanding in his monstrous predilections, refined in his perversions' (p. 212).

Myth

Flaubert wrote in a highly appreciative letter that Nana 'becomes mythic without ceasing to be a real woman'. The connotations of this comment are multiple: Nana's role as the Venus of vaudeville, the fact that she becomes the stuff of legend, and so on. Above all, Nana is 'mythic' in the sense that she is a construct of male sexual fantasies. Indeed, the men in the novel project onto her not only their fantasies but also their fears. She becomes a woman of fantastic proportions, incarnating the monsters of the male imagination. We most often see this monstrous Nana through the eyes of Comte Muffat, whose troubled gaze transforms Nana into a terrifying *femme fatale*. This is particularly pronounced in the scenes where she is naked. As Muffat watches her applying her make-up backstage at the Variétés, she is transformed into a devilish figure: 'In a confused way, Nana *was* the Devil, her laughter, her bosom, her bottom, she was swollen with vice' (p. 116). This nightmarish quality is most hysterical when Muffat, who has just read Faucherey's article allegorizing Nana as a disease-carrying fly, contemplates Nana's full nakedness as she stands preening herself before her bedroom mirror:

> Muffat followed that lovely profile, those glimpses of pink flesh sunk in a golden light, those silky curves in the reflections from the flames of the candles. He was remembering his former horror of woman, of the monster of Holy Scripture, lecherous, smelling like a wild animal. Nana was covered in fine hair, a reddish down turned her body into velvet, but in her thighs and rump, like those of a mare, in the fleshy slopes whose deep folds and furrows veiled her sex in a troubling shadow, there was something bestial. She was the golden beast, an unconscious force, the very scent of her could bring the world to ruin. Muffat, obsessed, possessed, went on staring, to the point where, having closed his lids so as not to see it any more, the animal loomed out of the darkness again, bigger, terrifying, even more menacing. (p. 171)

Through Muffat and his religiosity, Zola satirizes the doctrines and practices of a religion that sees all sex as Sin, and a type of 'cloying piety' (p. 322) embodied in the Muffats' oily spiritual confidant, Théophile Venot.

However, it is not only through the eyes of Muffat and his fantasies that we see Nana as the deadly sexual beast. The narrator, too, adopts this view of the heroine as the text progresses. There are moments when the narrator portrays Nana as a good-natured girl, but this generally occurs in scenes dominated by direct discourse, when Nana herself is talking. Increasingly, the narrator himself, when viewing the heroine, projects onto her fears similar to those of his male characters. 'Zola takes fright at his own creation,' suggests Peter Brooks. Symptomatically, the third-person narration in the penultimate chapter (chapter 13), when Nana reaches the height of her destructive powers, becomes fast and feverish. Representation of the mythic Nana, the man-eater, reaches a dizzy, hyperbolic pitch, as if she breaks free of all narratorial control. Her erotic body, the centre of the novel, becomes a vortex swallowing up men and their fortunes:

> Never had people seen such a crazy passion for spending money. The house seemed to be built over a bottomless pit, men and their possessions, their bodies, even their names were sucked into it without leaving so much as a speck of dust behind.   (p. 326)

Squandering money indiscriminately, Nana's capriciousness knows no bounds. She takes pleasure in destroying her lovers' gifts. The wastefulness of her household becomes surreal, a kind of gigantic haemorrhage. She allows the servants, presided over by the scheming Zoé, to siphon off her fortune, while creditors clamour over unpaid bills. One after the other, her lovers are devoured. Finally she turns to Faucherty's cousin La Faloise, whose fortune is in land: 'the tall grass which came up to the cows' bellies, it all disappeared, swallowed up in the abyss. And even a water-course, a stone quarry and three windmills had vanished down the hole. Nana passed like an invading army, like a cloud of locusts blazing through a province and stripping it. She scorched the earth wherever she put her dainty foot' (p. 348). At the end of the chapter, she stands alone, surrounded so to speak by the corpses of her victims: 'She stood alone in the midst of the piles of riches in her house with a whole host of men laid low at her feet. Like those monsters of old whose fearsome domains were littered in bones, she was treading on skulls' (p. 361).

As Peter Brooks has noted, Nana's sexuality, associated with heat and explosive energy, is the motor force of the narrative, functioning like the coal mine, the stock market, and the department store dramatized in Zola's other novels. Her frenzied consumption generates ever greater amounts of money, as her appetite for material goods increases. *Nana*, wrote Roland Barthes, is 'an epic book', not only because of the 'admirable excess' of its descriptions but also because of 'the very tempo of the work', its vertiginous rhythm: 'as the rot sets in, as the men are more and more tenaciously held in Nana's sway, the narrative gains speed and months at the end of the story are like minutes at the beginning'. The novel hurtles towards its end. The faster the engine goes, the more fuel it needs; it is fated to overheat, run out of control, and crash.

Just as Nana appears to break free of narratorial control, so the social and political symbolism she embodies becomes unstable. The idea of Nana as avenging angel of the working class, reflected in the image of a disease-carrying fly, is reintroduced at the end of chapter 13:

> Her work of ruin and death was over, the fly had flown off the dung heap of the faubourgs, bringing with it the ferment of social decay, and poisoning these men simply by alighting on them. It was good, it was just, she had avenged her own people, the beggars and the outcasts. And while sex rose triumphant in her and shone upon her prostrate victims like a rising sun lighting up a field of carnage, she remained as unconscious of it as a proud animal, ignorant of what she had wrought, always kind at heart. (p. 362)

But, as Bill Overton comments, 'Zola's portrayal of monstrous female sexuality in his heroine is so compulsive and excessive that it threatens to overwhelm the novel's entire critique of Empire society.' In the final chapter, describing Nana's death from smallpox as the chanting crowds surge past outside, the narrator seems to attribute the coming disaster not so much to the corruption of the Second Empire as to rampant female sexuality per se—something even more dreadful, it seems to be suggested, than the social wrongs Nana set out to avenge.

Chapter 6
The dream machine:
The Ladies' Paradise

The philandering Octave Mouret in *Pot Luck* (*Pot-Bouille*, 1882), Zola's ferociously comic picture of the hypocrisies pervading bourgeois life, uses sex to advance his career. In *The Ladies' Paradise* (serialized in the periodical *Gil Blas* and published in novel form by Charpentier in 1883) we see him using his charms on a mass scale to make his fortune as a businessman, as the quintessential Conquering Bourgeois who creates the world's first great department store. The novel is an important transitional text, for whereas *Pot Luck* had concentrated on the private lives of the bourgeoisie, its sequel marks Zola's desire to extend the scope of his work and embrace the whole of socio-economic reality; moreover, it contains a new, optimistic focus on the idea of 'progress'. *The Ladies' Paradise* is a celebration of modernity and the entrepreneurial spirit (Box 7). What he wanted to do in the novel, he declared in his planning notes, was 'write the poem of modern-day activity... In a word, go with our century, express our century, which is a century of action and conquest, of effort in every direction.'

Zola's store is modelled after the Bon Marché, Paris's first department store and the biggest department store in the world before 1914. Aristide Boucicaut (1810–77) took over the Bon Marché, a large drapery shop, in 1852 and quickly transformed it

Box 7 *The Ladies' Paradise*: a summary

The Ladies' Paradise depicts the Darwinian struggle between small retail businesses and the new phenomenon of the department store. The ruthless and enterprising Octave Mouret employs all the strategies of modern commerce to ensure the success of his store Au Bonheur des Dames. He plays especially on the susceptibilities of his middle-class female customers. The novel also tells the story of Denise Baudu, a young working-class woman from the provinces who comes to Paris and takes a job at the store as a sales assistant. She resists the advances of the normally irresistible Octave, who slowly falls in love with her. The novel ends with their marriage, a cooperative organization of the store being the price Denise puts on the marriage.

into a *grand magasin*. In 1852 it had four departments, twelve employees, and a turnover of 450,000 francs a year. By 1888 its turnover had risen to 123 million, and it occupied a whole city block. The establishment of the Bon Marché was followed by the founding of the BHV (Bazar de l'Hôtel de Ville) in 1854, the Grands Magasins du Louvre (usually just called Le Louvre) in 1855, Au Coin de la Rue in 1864, Au Printemps in 1865, La Belle Jardinière in 1866–7, La Samaritaine in 1869, and Les Galeries Lafayette in 1895 (Figure 9).

Consumer culture

The physical space of the store in Zola's novel is also social and cultural space. The store is a symbol of capitalism, the Second Empire, and the experience of the city; it is the site of 19th-century gender attitudes and class relations; and it is emblematic of new forms of consumer culture. The iron and glass-roofed shopping arcades, or *passages*, built during the Restoration (1814–30) and the reign of Louis Philippe (1830–48), were places for the display

9. The Galeries Lafayette. The most iconic Parisian department store is situated on the Boulevard Haussmann in the 9th *arrondissement*. In 1895, Théophile Bader and Alphonse Kahn took over a small haberdasher's shop at the corner of Rue La Fayette and the Chaussée d'Antin. In 1896, their company purchased the entire building at 1 Rue La Fayette; in 1905 they acquired the buildings at 38, 40, and 42 Boulevard Haussmann and 15 Rue de la Chaussée d'Antin. Bader commissioned the architect Georges Chedanne and his pupil Ferdinand Chanut to design the store at the Haussmann location, where a glass and steel dome and Art Nouveau staircases were finished in 1912. Zola's descriptions of the interior of the store in *The Ladies' Paradise* anticipate these developments.

and sale of commodities, which they enshrined in visions of abundance and luxury. The development during the Second Empire of the department stores (which made use of the same iron and glass structures that were used for the arcades) marked a significant development in the growth of consumer culture. If commodities had earlier promised to fulfil human desires, now they created them: dreams themselves became commodities. In the 1850s Boucicaut developed a new retailing policy. He realized that, whereas he could make a living from supplying a conscious need on the part of the customers, he could make an infinitely better living by supplying a desire the customer did not know she had until she entered the shop. In this way, Boucicaut pioneered the idea of the department store as a building purposely designed for fashionable public assembly and which, by the use of display techniques, eye-catching design, and other ploys, replaced the principle of commercial supply with that of consumer seduction.

The mechanisms of seduction, all of which are described in detail in *The Ladies' Paradise*, were multiple. They included advertising (an entirely novel practice at the time); 'free entry' (the freedom to enter the shop and browse without being obliged to buy, by which shopping came to be seen for the first time as a leisure activity); fixed prices (which fostered speed and impersonality of purchase); a system of 'returns' (the easy exchangeability of purchases that failed to satisfy); and, of course, sales. In addition, there was the manipulation of space—the creation of deliberate disorder, disconnection, in the internal layout of the store. This obliged the shoppers to travel the length and breadth of the shop to find items they had come to purchase; as they walked through the shop, they were exposed to other items they had not initially intended to buy. Above all, there was the seduction of pure spectacle, the seduction of the eye through an almost orgiastic display of commodities. The shop windows were organized to entice potential customers (mainly women) to come into the store. Octave Mouret is presented as the best window dresser in Paris. Window shopping along the boulevards became a standard form of Parisian *flânerie*. The term 'window shopping' in French is suggestively sensual: 'lèche-vitrines'—literally, licking windows. The department store sold not just commodities, but the very process of consumption, transforming the mundane activity of shopping into a pleasurable experience.

The department store as spectacle was part of the general spectacularization of the city by Baron Haussmann. It was not simply a question of the monumentality of the new urban architecture, but of a general culture of the spectacle: of flamboyant, celebratory modernity. The new boulevards created their own forms of spectacle as centres of public display; and, as David Harvey has written in his invaluable book *Paris, Capital of Modernity*:

> Their theatricality fused with the performative world inside the many theaters, cafés, and other places of entertainment that sprang up along them to create spaces for the display of bourgeois affluence, conspicuous consumption, and feminine fashion. The boulevards, in short, became spaces where the fetish of the commodity reigned supreme.

The first view of the giant store is presented through the uplifted eyes of Denise Baudu, freshly arrived from the provinces:

> Denise felt she was watching a machine working at high pressure, its dynamism seeming to reach to the display windows themselves...There was the continuous roar of the machine at work, of customers crowding into the departments, dazzled by the merchandise, then propelled towards the cash-desk. And it was all regulated and organized with the remorselessness of a machine: the vast horde of women were as if caught in the wheels of an inevitable force. (p. 16)

Mouret's machine is a model and a metaphor for the new form of capitalism: that is, an economic system based on the principle of circulation, movement, turnover, the constant and increasingly rapid renewal of capital in the form of commodities. The descriptions of the sales, with their swirling movement and their frenetic circulation of money, goods, and bodies, are the perfect expression of commodity culture, which is a culture of speed, movement, and disorientation.

> The great afternoon rush-hour had arrived, when the overheated machine led the dance of customers, extracting money from their very flesh. In the silk department especially there was a sense of madness... In the still air, where the stifling central heating brought out the smell of the materials, the hubbub was increasing, made up of all sorts of noises—the continuous trampling of feet, the same phrases repeated a hundred times at the counters, gold clinking on the brass of the cash-desks besieged by a mass of purses, the baskets on wheels with their loads of parcels falling endlessly into the gaping cellars... (pp. 108–9)

Mouret's success is due not only to his refined understanding of the capitalist system, but also to his exploitation of another new system, namely, the integrated transportation network which facilitated the rapid circulation of goods both within the city and between Paris and the rest of the world. Two basic elements of the new transportation system were the railway (by the end of the Second Empire six new railway lines converged on the capital) and Baron Haussmann's new network of boulevards. Haussmann's massive redevelopment of the city by means of broad, straight, strategically placed boulevards forestalled the erecting of barricades and facilitated the movement of troops, reflecting the counter-revolutionary needs of the Emperor; but its aim was also to advance the bourgeoisie's business interests by creating a more efficient transportation network. Mouret longs to expand his operation so that The Ladies' Paradise will have its entrance and a spectacular new frontage on one of the grand new boulevards, the Rue du Dix-Décembre (renamed in 1870 the Rue du

Quatre-Septembre). He thus curries favour with the man in charge of the redevelopment, Baron Hartmann, whose name, with its obvious resemblance to Haussmann, is clearly no coincidence. Mouret tries to convince the Baron to develop a section of the new boulevard with an extension of the department store. If he could have found a way, the narrator tells us, 'he would have made the street run right through his shop' (p. 236). He succeeds, in a sense, in doing this by the visual openness created by his use of sheet glass and electric lighting for his ground-floor window displays, and by his system of interior traffic circulation which is modelled on Haussmann's network of boulevards. Again it is pertinent to note that the department store, the Second Empire, and the modernization of Paris by Haussmann all form part of the same general economy. Mouret's ability to use the interior space of his store to his own advantage, so that he can dominate his female subjects, mirrors Louis-Napoleon's enhanced ability to control potential insurgents by means of his new boulevards. Similarly, just as Haussmann's opening up of Paris improved the commercial capacity of the city, so Mouret is able to provide a dynamic retail environment by opening up the space of the store, in contrast to the cramped darkness of the old drapery shops.

Women and shopping

One of the significant features of the 19th-century department store is that it showed women emerging more and more into the public spaces of the city. Bourgeois women were largely excluded from 19th-century urban space, while bourgeois men were free to explore urban zones of pleasure such as the restaurant, the theatre, the café, and the brothel. The proliferation of public places of pleasure and leisure created a new kind of public person: the *flâneur*, a key figure in the critical literature of modernity and urbanization (see Box 4). Shopping in the late 19th century became a woman's natural way of entering into and occupying the public domain, though the pleasures of shopping were not available to all women—largely for reasons of class. Whereas for upper- and middle-class women the department store was the equivalent of the arcades, a protected place half-way between the home and the street, for working-class women the store was hardly different from the street: whether in the street or in the store, Denise and the other working-class salesgirls are constantly a prey, because of their subordinate social and economic status, to the masculine gaze; and they themselves are also buyable objects. But for the leisured few, shopping provided the pleasures of looking, socializing, and simply strolling; in the department store a woman, too, could become a *flâneur*. As orthodox religion had once instructed women in the moral codes of daily life, so the department store now delineated a new religion of femininity and womanhood. The store offered a world in which they could enjoy a sense of freedom from the routines of domesticity and family life.

However, although women enjoyed the new culture of the commodity, they were themselves commodified. Mouret, always a figure of power, is not only a kind of capitalist emperor; he is also the Great Seducer: 'Mouret's sole passion was the conquest of Woman' (p. 234). His talent is to arouse and orchestrate consumer desire (Box 8).

The shop, objects, things, are eroticized, transforming everything for sale into an object of desire. The store becomes not only a kind of harem but a dream machine, generating limitless sensual fantasies. The rhythmic structure of the descriptions, with their cascading images and rising pitch, suggests loss of control, the female shoppers' quasi-sexual abandonment to consumer desire.

> At the far end of the hall, around one of the small cast-iron columns which supported the glass roof, material was streaming down like a bubbling sheet of water, falling from above and spreading out on to the floor ... Women pale with desire were leaning over as if to look at themselves. Faced with this wild cataract, they all just stood there, filled with the secret fear of being caught in the overflow of

Box 8 The conquest of Woman

Of supreme importance was the exploitation of women. Everything led up to it: the ceaseless renewal of capital, the system of piling up the merchandise, the low prices to attract the customers, the fixed prices to reassure them. It was Woman the shops were competing for so fiercely, it was Woman they were continually snaring with their bargains, after dazzling her with their displays. They had aroused new desires in her flesh, they were a huge temptation to which she inevitably succumbed, giving in first of all to purchases for the house, then seduced by coquetry, and finally consumed by desire. By increasing their sales tenfold, by democratizing luxury, the shops were becoming terrible agents for spending, ravaging households, working hand in hand with the latest extravagances in fashion, growing ever more expensive... 'Get the women,' he said... laughing suggestively, 'and you'll sell the world.'

(*The Ladies' Paradise*, pp. 76–7, translation modified. Octave Mouret is explaining 'the techniques of modern business' to Baron Hartmann.)

all this luxury and with an irresistible desire to throw themselves into it and be lost. (pp. 103–4)

The women shoppers themselves are shown as fragmented, reduced to distorted parts of the body, merged with the fabrics and objects in the shop, like modern advertising images:

the mirrors made the departments recede further into the distance, reflecting the displays together with patches of the public—faces in reverse, bits of shoulders and arms. (p. 250)

Furthermore, the vocabulary of sexual dominance and exploitation is accompanied by images marked by a great deal of violence directed against women. On the way up the staircase of

The Ladies' Paradise there is a curious and disturbing image of rows of headless mannequins:

> each one had a little wooden handle like the handle of a dagger, stuck in the red flannel, which seemed to be bleeding where the neck had been severed.   (p. 253)

The first window display Denise sees when she arrives in Paris features a row of mannequins, mirrored to infinity, with price tags instead of heads. The women shoppers lose their heads in that they undergo a euphoric loss of self; they go mad in ecstasies of buying, succumbing in spectacular fashion to false consciousness. In that sense they become mere bodies, manipulated and mindless.

The description of the mannequins focuses the commodity fetishism, with its attendant sense of hysteria, that figures so prominently in the novel. The women shoppers have an erotic fascination with the commodity objects in Mouret's store. After the first of the three great sales (each the focus of an extended bravura description), the lace and lingerie scattered on the floors and counters 'gave the impression that an army of women had undressed there haphazardly in a wave of desire' (p. 117). An endless array of underwear seems strewn everywhere during the climactic scene of the final chapter, 'as if an army of pretty girls had undressed as they went from department to department, down to their satiny skin'. The mannequins themselves seem to have a 'disturbing lewdness' (p. 409).

Denise Baudu

In opposition to Mouret stands Denise Baudu, the young working-class girl who is often seen as the feminist pole of the novel, the representative of the women and the workers. Denise is the only one of the salesgirls who refuses to be commodified; having refused Mouret's advances, she wins his heart. But the price of her hand in marriage is the introduction of humanitarian reforms in the running of the store, which depends on a brutal system of labour organization. The role of Denise is thus to humanize the store, to harmonize its economic functions with the moral qualities associated with femininity. The novel's romance plot has been read by feminist critics as an allegory of female revenge and the achievement of autonomy; but what is more striking is the bourgeois ideology, the enduring patriarchal structure, that informs the domestication of Mouret. Although Denise breaks the mould of masculine domination, her influence and independence are achieved only in terms of her critical presence within the existing system. The novel relates, after all, her gradual acceptance of 'the logical development of business, the needs of modern times, the magnitude of these new creations, and finally the increasing well-being of the public' (p. 210). She argues for her reforms in the spirit of sound business practice, and in rewriting Mouret's male narrative of sexual and economic exploitation, she uses the discourse of bourgeois ideology—the discourse of reason, logic, control, and order:

> She could never do anything herself, or watch any job being done, without being obsessed with the need to put method into it, to improve the system...She would plead the cause of the cogs in this great machine, not for sentimental reasons, but with arguments based on the employers' own interests.   (p. 355)

The domestication of Mouret is identified, moreover, with an idealization of the bourgeois family, the final figuration of the store; and the bourgeois family becomes the social family, indeed the corporate family. Michael Miller, in his book on the Bon Marché, writes:

> In the Bon Marché vision there was no place for class discord or conflict, no place for that nagging bourgeois nightmare that its century of change, with all its conglomeration of money and men, might be carrying within it the seeds of its collapse. The Bon

Marché world was a harmonious blend of order, authority, cooperation, and social unity.

At the beginning, the store is seen as a threat to the family, that is, to the small family businesses it swallows up; but in the end the family is restored, so to speak, in a form better adapted to the new capitalism—in the form of Octave and Denise, the capitalist and the worker united as man and wife, watching paternally over their huge, happy family of employees.

Chapter 7
Down the mine: *Germinal*

The Commune had persuaded Zola that his Rougon-Macquart series should include a novel devoted to revolutionary activity in a contemporary setting. At the beginning of his planning notes for *Germinal*, he wrote:

> The subject of the novel is the revolt of the workers, the jolt given to society, which for a moment cracks: in a word, the struggle between capital and labour. There lies the importance of the book, which I want to show predicting the future, putting the question that will be the most important question of the twentieth century.

The question of class conflict, barely touched on in *L'Assommoir*, is the main theme of *Germinal*. In *L'Assommoir* Zola had used narrative technique, and narrative voice in particular, to make articulate the inarticulate—to make us see and hear the world through the workers' eyes and voices. In *Germinal*, he does something similar; but in the later novel he also depicts a moment in history when the workers begin to find a political voice (Box 9).

The action of *Germinal* is set in 1867–8, but its treatment is coloured by political developments between the closing years of the Second Empire and the mid-1880s, when Zola wrote his novel. Socialist ideas became more widespread. The International

Box 9 *Germinal*: a summary

The novel is the story of a strike in a mining community in the north of France. The protagonist is Étienne Lantier, the youngest son of Gervaise Macquart and her lover Lantier from *L'Assommoir*. An unemployed railwayman, he finds work in a mine in the town of Montsou. Horrified by the inhuman working and living conditions of the miners, he organizes a strike against the mining company. The strike turns violent and government troops fire on the workers, who eventually return to work, blaming Étienne for the failure of the strike. A Russian anarchist, Souvarine, sabotages the entrance shaft of one of the pits, trapping Étienne and others at the bottom. Miraculously saved, Étienne leaves Montsou for Paris to continue the struggle on behalf of the workers.

(the International Workingmen's Association) had been formed in 1864; a French socialist party was launched in 1879, under the leadership of Jules Guesde (1845–1922), a defender of the Commune who in 1877 had returned to Paris from exile in Geneva. Many of the exiled or deported Communards had also returned to France. Russian anarchists had achieved particular notoriety, notably with the assassination of the Tsar Alexander II in 1881 and the widely publicized trial of Peter Kropotkin in Lyon on a bomb-throwing charge in 1882. Trade unions, prohibited earlier, were legalized in 1884. Large-scale strikes had taken place in French coal mines since the last years of the Second Empire. In June 1869 at La Ricamarie (near Saint-Étienne), troops fired on striking workers, killing thirteen, including a pregnant woman and a child; in October of the same year, a similar confrontation at Aubin (in the Aveyron) left fourteen dead. There had been serious strikes in northern France, near the Belgian border: at Anzin in 1878, Denain in 1880, and Montceau-les-Mines in 1882. Miners' groups and socialist deputies were vigorously lobbying the government to improve the working conditions of miners.

LES HOMMES DU JOUR. — par LUQUE

L'auteur de " Germinal ", M. ÉMILE ZOLA.

Down the mine: *Germinal*

10. A cartoon by Luque (*La Caricature*, 1885). This cartoon evokes
Zola's immersion, in terms of his preparatory work for his novels, in
the social worlds he depicts. In February 1884 he spent a week in a
mining community in north-eastern France. With notebook in hand,
he recorded all that he observed and needed for *Germinal*. He took
more than a hundred sheets of notes, exploring the area above and
below ground. Most strikingly, he recorded his impressions on
descending into one of the pits, the Fosse Renard, recording the
miners' tasks at the coal face and their general conditions of work.

During the summer of 1883, while on holiday in Brittany, Zola met one such campaigner, Alfred Giard, an extreme left-wing deputy for Valenciennes, close to Anzin. He had begun preparing *Germinal*, and Giard had invited him to visit the Valenciennes region, when a major strike broke out on 21 February 1884 near Anzin, involving 12,000 men. Four days later Zola rushed up to the coalfields and spent a week, posing as the deputy's secretary, taking copious notes on everything he saw and heard. He even mastered his fear of the dark and of being buried alive to go down the Renard mine near Denain, stumbling along labyrinthine tunnels, recording impressions that would be passed on to Étienne Lantier when he first goes down the mine (Figure 10).

A figure in a dream

The novel is both a graphically realistic representation of the miners' lives and a work of commanding imaginative power, a distinctive mixture of realism and poetry, authentic detail and hallucinatory vision. The vehicle, structurally, of the novel's documentary realism, poetic effects, and thematic development is the protagonist, Étienne, the outsider who, in the opening chapter, arrives in Montsou at dead of night. He is both a seeing eye and, later, a catalyst of the action. To the newcomer everything is new and strange. As he trudges through the eerie, frozen landscape things appear as in a dream or nightmare. Suddenly he comes upon the mine, which looms out of the darkness, lit by strange fires:

> The pit, with its squat brick buildings crammed together at the
> bottom of a hollow, and its chimney sticking up like a menacing
> horn, seemed to have the sinister air of a ravenous beast crouching
> ready to gobble everyone up.

Étienne begins to talk with a ghostly old man, a haulier named Maheu but nicknamed Bonnemort, as he stands by a brazier warming his hands. Étienne asks the old man who owns the mine. The old man coughs, spits out black coal-dust, and says:

Box 10 Descent into Hell

The four hewers had just spread themselves out, each lying at a different height, so as to cover the whole expanse of the coal-face. They were separated by boards, hung on hooks, which caught the coal as they hewed it away; they each worked over about four metres of the seam at a time; and the seam was so thin, hardly more than half a metre thick at that point, that they were more or less flattened between the roof and the wall, dragging themselves around on their knees and elbows, unable to turn round without bruising their shoulders. In order to get at the coal, they had to stay stretched out on one side, with their necks twisted, so that they could swing their arms far enough back to wield their short-handled picks at an angle...

It was Maheu who had the worst of it... To see what he was doing, he had had to hang his lamp on a nail just above his head, and after a while its heat set his blood on fire. But it was the dampness that really tortured him. The rock above him was just a few centimetres away from his face and big drops of water streamed from it incessantly, falling with maddening regularity, always on the same spot... The darkness seemed unnaturally black, thick with swirling coal-dust and heavy with gases that pressed down on their eyes... Ghostly figures could be seen moving about, as an occasional gleam threw into relief an arched hip, a sinewy arm, or a grim face, daubed and dirty as if in preparation for some crime. Sometimes, as a block of coal was dislodged, its surface or corners would suddenly sparkle like crystal. Then everything would be plunged into darkness again...

(*Germinal*, part I, chapter 4)

'What? Who does it belong to? God knows...People...'

And he pointed in the darkness to some distant, unknown place, where these people lived, for whom the Maheu family had been hacking away at the seam for over a century.

His voice had taken on a kind of religious awe, as though he were speaking of some inaccessible tabernacle, which concealed the crouching, greedy god to whom they all offered up their flesh, but whom they had never seen.

'Religious awe': the miners are, in the Marxist sense, alienated. That is to say, they sense how unbearable their situation is, but, as labourers within the capitalist mode of production, they have no clear understanding of its material causes and are unable to conceive of themselves as the agents of their own actions. Free-enterprise capitalism, embodied in the mining company, is presented as a remote idol, an alien entity, to be propitiated by human subservience and sacrifice. Just as the pithead is transformed metaphorically into an insatiable monster, so descent into the depths of the mine, the symbolic centre of the novel, is seen as descent into Hell (Box 10).

A scarlet vision

Among the many artistic qualities of *Germinal* are its use of colour and its strong light-and-dark contrasts. The two dominant colours are black (the landscape of the coal-mining country, the underground world of the mine, the darkness of ignorance and misery) and red (associated with revolution). In the first half of the novel, black dominates; in the second half, red. The description of the striking miners rampaging across the countryside in part V, chapter 5, is saturated in red. The last rays of the sun turn the plain blood-red, the road seems 'awash with blood', and the men and women in the mob seem soaked in blood, like 'butchers in a slaughter-house'. The miners' rhythmic cry, 'Bread! We want bread!'; the singing of the Marseillaise (first composed during the

French Revolution and banned under the Second Empire); and the single axe, held above their heads 'like the blade of a guillotine'—these details evoke the bloody events of 1789–94. 'It was a scarlet vision,' writes Zola, 'of the revolution that would inevitably carry them all away, on some blood-soaked fin de siècle evening.'

It is important to note that this 'scarlet vision', with its images of the workers' bestialization, is essentially an instance of free indirect discourse, reflecting the fears of a bourgeoisie nurtured on memories of the Commune—for the scene is presented through the eyes of a group of bourgeois characters who have taken refuge in a barn. As the mob surges past, fear of socialism is transformed in the bourgeois mind into apocalyptic terror, reflecting the perception of the threatened class, which equates the threat to their privileged position with the end of civilization itself:

> That was it, one night the people would rise up, cast caution aside, and run riot like this far and wide all over the countryside; and there would be rivers of bourgeois blood, their heads would be waved on pikes, their strong-boxes hacked open, and their gold poured all over the ground…There would be nothing left, not a sou of inherited wealth, not a line of legal entitlement…That was the future out there, tearing down the road like some natural disaster, and buffeting their faces with its great hurricane wind.

Through his description of the strike, Zola evokes and celebrates the awakening of the miners' political consciousness—movingly with Maheu's finding of a voice when the delegation of miners goes to see the mine manager, Hennebeau; hypnotically with Bonnemort's inarticulate but nerve-tingling 'speech' during the midnight meeting in the forest. But the strike eventually collapses. The miners' plight at the end of the novel is even worse than at the beginning. The description of them trudging back to work is juxtaposed, however, with the resounding rhetoric of the last few paragraphs, the free indirect discourse describing Étienne's thoughts as he strides away to catch the train to Paris to join Pluchart, an organizer of the International, and imagines he can hear the sound of picks prophesying victory. The novel's final sentence, with its reference to 'a black avenging army of men', like seeds 'thrusting upwards in readiness for harvests to come, until one day soon their ripening would burst open the earth itself', looks forward to a final day of reckoning. It must be stressed, however, that the optimism of the ending is that of Étienne. The ending remains ambiguous.

A plurality of voices

The novel's ambiguity can be seen in particularly sharp relief if we consider it from the perspective of the theme of leadership. *Germinal* is a study in the problems of working-class leadership as well as a study in the dynamics of collective action. Both the innkeeper Rasseneur and the activist Pluchart are portrayed as vain and self-centred. As for Étienne, at one level the novel is the story of his political education. In the novel's concluding chapter we read: 'His education was complete, he was going forth fully armed as a fighting missionary of the revolution…' We see his initial sense of the horror of the miners' life, and we see his slow political awakening. But Zola also shows the limitations of his education—his muddled thinking, his patchy reading. His socialism is portrayed as a jumble of incompatible dogmas picked up haphazardly from Marx, Proudhon, and others. And Zola stresses the insidious attraction of popularity, power, and bourgeois values once he establishes a position of authority over his fellow workers. Having discovered a rhetorical talent, he becomes a demagogue, defeating the moderate Rasseneur. But he is the victim of his own success in that he unleashes a force he is unable to control. The miners' collective disintegrates into a violent mob, and Étienne gradually loses contact with the men for whom he wished to speak.

How revolting they were, these wretches piled one on top of the other, washing in each other's dirty water! Not one of them could hold a serious political conversation, they lived just like cattle...Gradually his vanity at being their leader and his constant concern to think on their behalf were detaching him from them, and creating in him the soul of one of those bourgeois he so hated.

(part VI, chapter 1)

Just as Étienne, Rasseneur, and Souvarine—the militant, the moderate, and the anarchist—represent in broad terms three strands of the labour movement, so we have three representatives of the capitalist system: Hennebeau, the ex-miner become manager; Deneulin, the owner of a small colliery; and the Grégoires, the shareholders, placidly smug and atrociously ignorant of the reality they are living off. The political ambiguity of the novel is compounded by the fact that the bourgeois representatives of capitalism are far from being uniformly unsympathetic. Zola stresses the divided responsibilities of Hennebeau, trapped by economic circumstance. But the most sympathetic bourgeois is the progressive, hard-working Deneulin. Like Hennebeau's nephew Négrel, Deneulin is respected for his energy and courage. Though authoritarian and paternalistic, he is an excellent manager of men; and he is allied with the miners not only through the compassion he shows towards them but through the fact that, like them, he is crushed by the big company of Montsou. Although Zola wished to base his novel on stark contrasts, the bourgeoisie is not presented as monolithic; there are contrasts within the bourgeoisie as well as between the classes. The contrast between the idle Grégoires and the enlightened Deneulin emerges with particular clarity at the great dinner held at La Piolaine, the Grégoires' house, to celebrate the engagement of Cécile and Négrel after the failure of the strike. The dinner quickly turns into a celebration of the victory over the miners: the smugness of the Grégoires is contrasted with the melancholy of Deneulin, whom the strike has ruined. Zola laments the triumph of conservatism and egoism, juxtaposing the defeat of the man of energy with the self-congratulation of the parasites.

Germinal thus contains a plurality of political voices. The implied optimism of the ending, with its suggestion that the revolt of the Montsou miners has been exemplary, and its image of the germination of a new social order, is belied by Zola's scepticism towards revolutionary activity and his devaluation of Étienne as a leader. There is a disjunction, moreover, between the treatment of social conflict in contingent, historical terms (located in a particular place at a particular moment in history, and involving particular ideologies and political choices) and its representation in timeless, mythic terms (the class struggle seen as pertaining to the natural order and the emergence of the revolutionary proletariat seen as a Darwinian necessity). The novel brings out the depth of contemporary social problems in a way that exploits the fears of its bourgeois readers, and Zola shows as no novelist before him the emergence of a new historical force and the conflict that must follow; but the outcome remains ambiguous.

What is extremely clear, however, is that Zola wished to deploy all the resources of his craft—poetic, epic, symphonic—to communicate his sense of the brutality of industrial capitalism. *Germinal* is a compelling depiction of exploitation, conceived as a dramatic warning to the dominant classes. In an interview with the newspaper Le Matin, he was quoted as saying:

> At the risk of being labelled a socialist, I must tell you that when I saw how miners lived, pity overwhelmed me. My book is a work of pity, nothing else, and if readers experience this feeling, I shall be happy…There is a great social movement afoot, a desire for justice that must be taken seriously, or bourgeois society will be swept away.

Chapter 8
The Great Mother: *Earth*

Earth (*La Terre*, 1887) has always been recognized as one of Zola's finest and most characteristic achievements. When he embarked on it, he declared that he felt it would be his favourite among his novels. Its hallmark, in keeping with the naturalist aesthetic, is the representation of the peasants as they really were—in sharp contrast to the idealized representations of rural life by novelists like George Sand (1804–76) and painters like Jean-François Millet (1814–75). The peasants' existence is harsh, their mentality primitive and insular, their attachment to the land savage to the point of murderous violence (Box 11). Zola's story exploded the myth, so deeply embedded in the nation's cultural psyche, of 'the simple goodness of the peasants'. David Baguley has pointed out that Zola's grimly realistic depiction of rural life may be read in specifically literary terms: in terms of the novelist's construction of a text that is, parodically and ironically, anti-pastoral. The novel's protagonist, Jean Macquart, a stranger to the rural community depicted, had entertained thoughts of retiring to the country, but

> how silly of him to imagine that, when he laid down his rifle and his plane, the plough would satisfy his desire for peace and quiet! If the earth was restful, and good to those who loved it, the villages that clung to it like nests of vermin, the human insects that lived off its flesh, were enough to dishonour it and blight any contact with it.
>
> (pp. 357–8)

Box 11 *Earth*: a summary

The novel is set in the village of Rognes in the Beauce, the great wheat-growing region south-west of Paris. The plot revolves round the fate of an old peasant smallholder, Fouan, who, like Shakespeare's King Lear, divides his land between his three adult children: Hyacinthe, a lazy, drunken poacher known as 'Jesus Christ'; Fanny, the prim wife of a prosperous landowner, Delhomme; and Jules, known as 'Buteau'. In exchange, they agree to pay him a monthly pension and supply him and his wife with certain provisions. But once he has handed over his land, he loses his authority and his children fail to keep their part of the bargain. He sells his house and moves in with each of them in turn. With each move he is treated with increasing brutality. Like Lear, he is humiliated and rejected by his children; and his last days are spent, not in madness, but in physical and mental despair. Meanwhile, Fouan's niece Françoise, who lives with the Buteaus, has become involved with Jean Macquart, a former soldier and carpenter who now works as a farmhand. Françoise demands her share of her inheritance, including the land she owns with her sister Lise, and she subsequently marries Jean. A bitter feud ensues. When Françoise falls pregnant, the Buteaus are enraged, since the birth of an heir will take the land out of the family. Buteau, helped by Lise, brutally rapes Françoise to prevent the child from being born. Lise attacks her sister with a scythe. The child is lost and Françoise dies, refusing to name her attackers and leaving no will, impelled to the last by an atavistic sense of family loyalty. The crime is silently observed by Fouan, and the Buteaus resolve to kill him too. They smother him in his bed and set him on fire. Jean guesses what has happened, but, out of respect for Françoise's last wishes, does nothing. Realizing that he will always be an outsider (like Étienne Lantier in *Germinal*, cast out of the mining community as an unwanted intruder), he decides to rejoin the army and leaves the Beauce forever.

Zola's dark vision of the peasant world, existing beyond all civilized values, and the prominence in his novel of explicit sex and bodily functions, provoked an uproar. It brought to the fore once again the controversy that had always informed critical responses to naturalism. After the *succès de scandale* of *Thérèse Raquin*, there had been the furore surrounding *L'Assommoir*. Now, ten years after *L'Assommoir*, came the moral outrage that greeted *Earth*. The most widely read expression of this outrage was the so-called 'Manifesto of the Five'. Published on 18 August 1887 in *Le Figaro*, the day Zola finished the novel but while it was still appearing in serial form, this 'manifesto' (probably instigated, for reasons of jealousy, by Zola's fellow novelists Edmond de Goncourt and Alphonse Daudet) was a vicious attack on the novel and on Zola personally. It was signed by five young authors claiming to represent the younger generation of writers: Paul Bonnetain, J.-H. Rosny, Lucien Descaves, Paul Margueritte, and Gustave Guiches. Zola's 'violent penchant for obscenity', they wrote, was a symptom of his 'insatiable appetite for sales' and of his own psychological and physical dysfunction ('the illness of his loins'). In sum, *Earth* was nothing but 'a collection of scatological stories' in which the Master had sunk to the lowest depths of vulgarity. In similar vein, the well-known novelist Anatole France denounced the novel in *Le Temps* as 'the Georgics of Filth', while the establishment critic Ferdinand Brunetière, writing in the *Revue des deux mondes*, took advantage of the manifesto to proclaim the naturalist movement bankrupt.

A poem of the Earth

Zola's aim in the novel, he wrote, was to paint a comprehensive picture of the French peasantry, 'with their history, their mores, their role...With *La Terre* I would like to do for the peasant what I did for the worker with *Germinal*.' It is important to note the significance of Zola's subject in relation to his desire to write a 'social history' of contemporary France: France in the 19th century was predominantly a country of villages; in 1871 the rural population made up two-thirds of the population as a whole. The novel's panorama of rural France includes a large and varied cast of characters: peasant smallholders, a shepherd, farmhands, labourers, a poacher, a gamekeeper, innkeepers (one also a grocer, the other a tobacco dealer), a large-scale tenant farmer, a factory owner, an absentee landlord, a doctor, a vet, a notary, a tax-collector, a schoolteacher, and two long-suffering parish priests. Politics, both national and local, is amply covered, with an evocation of ongoing debates about protectionism versus free trade in the context of legislative elections, and a description of a meeting of the local municipal council and the selection of a new mayor.

Zola embarked on his usual programme of research before settling down to write the novel. He consulted several general works on the history of French agriculture, one of which formed the basis of the extended historical account of the French peasantry: the 'Jacques Bonhomme' section of part I, chapter 5, where Jean Macquart reads to the assembled peasants a pamphlet that traces their history from feudal serfdom to the Revolution of 1789. Zola was particularly impressed by the written reflections (*Pensées*, 1886) of a country priest named Joseph Roux on his parishioners in a village in the Corrèze—mean and grasping peasants similar to those depicted by Zola.

On 2 May 1886 Zola had lunch, arranged by his friend Paul Alexis, with the socialist writer and activist Jules Guesde, leader of the French Workers' Party, who had published a number of articles on rural economic questions. Guesde sharpened Zola's insights into the main reasons for the agricultural crisis that had afflicted the nation since the late 1870s, when competition from abroad, especially the importation of cheap wheat from the United States, began to drive the grain price down. The issues underlying this crisis (which was to last until the mid-1890s) are the subject of recurrent discussion or allusion in the novel: the ever-increasing subdivision of the land because of the French system of inheritance, the flight of capital into industry, lack of credit, labour shortages, deficiencies of agricultural education, and the conservatism of the French peasant, unwilling (unlike the progressive farmer Hourdequin) to adopt modern farming methods. According to Guesde, the only solution lay in the mechanization of agriculture and the collectivization of the land through full nationalization. His views are reflected in the novel in those of the revolutionary, Canon, and, to a certain extent, Jesus Christ and the anarchistic schoolteacher, Lequeu.

The day after his meeting with Guesde, Zola and his wife Alexandrine set off on a week-long field trip to the Beauce, travelling around the countryside in a two-horse landau. He attended a big cattle market, visited farms, conducted interviews, and took extensive notes. This research undoubtedly informed the remarkable particularity of authentic detail that informs his depiction of the peasants' world, as well as his elaboration of scenes that evoke 'the eternal round of things' (p. 118): the evening gatherings in the cowshed, weddings, baptisms, fairs, funerals, as well as the sowing, haymaking, and harvesting. However, it did not alter (but rather, reinforced) his imaginative conception of the reality he wished to depict. The first line of his planning notes for the novel, written before he undertook his research work, indicates his literary intentions: 'I want to write a poem of the Earth.' It is Zola's poetic vision in *Earth*, magisterially combining realism, lyricism, tragedy, comedy, and myth, that gives the novel its power, its texture, and its shape. The novel's central character, Zola wrote, is Earth, the Great Mother herself: 'A gigantic character, always present, filling the entire book.'

The land and the body

The central theme of the novel is the peasants' obsession with land ownership and acquisition. Their property constitutes their identity. Fouan's name, derived from the verbs *fouir* and *enfouir* (to dig, to bury), reflects his passionate attachment to the land, 'a passion that can only be described as lust' (p. 18). Zola continually uses the metaphor of land as a woman. Buteau, the 'lover' of the land, 'wanted to force his way into it and fertilize it deep inside' (p. 161), while Hourdequin, the bourgeois farmer with extensive holdings, bitterly recognizes his enslavement: 'When the bloody land gets its claws into you, it never lets go…' (p. 125). Both attitudes could be transposed to the two men's experiences with women. Buteau, lusting to possess, sees women's bodies as the means to slake his desire; what he wants, he takes. Hourdequin is manipulated by a servant girl, who sees the ultimate prize as the transfer of her body from the narrow servant's bed to the four-poster of the farmer's dead wife. The female body also becomes a signifier of land ownership, to be taken when necessary in marriage. Buteau is the archetypal rural male, embodiment of the peasant's single-minded will to possess. His name has the same second syllable as *taureau* (bull), while the first syllable evokes *buté* (pig-headed). His marriage to Lise formalizes a liaison which has already produced a bastard son. However, it is not fatherhood that motivates him to marry, but Lise's acquisition of some valuable land. Moreover, her land adjoins his, therefore her body must naturally assume the same position vis-à-vis his. Buteau also lusts after his sister-in-law, Françoise, all too aware of her value, too, as inheritor of land. Family ties are thus inherently compromised. Landless parents become superfluous, while brothers, sisters, and cousins become competitors, agents of the dispersal and disintegration of property.

In ironic counterpoint to the fractious Fouans stands the hypocritical but harmonious Charles family. The only local who has turned away from that fickle mistress the land, Monsieur Charles (Fouan's brother-in-law) has put his money into the more dependable complaisance of the female body in the form of a brothel in Chartres, turning it into a thriving establishment for the cream of local society. A source of great pride, this property affords them entry to the bourgeoisie, an idyllic country retreat for their old age, and the money to pay for the superior education of their daughter and granddaughter in the virginal enclosure of a convent school. In a parodic display of bourgeois enlightenment, their granddaughter Élodie follows in the footsteps of her mother (who has died of overwork) by asking, after blushingly accepting a fiancé, if she may take over the management of the brothel, the 'sweetshop' of whose existence her grandparents had been at such pains to keep her ignorant and which, as a gilt-edged concern, should clearly not be allowed to pass out of the family. The description of the Charleses, though cast in a different mode (comedy) from that of their peasant neighbours, tells the same essential story ('blood will out', p. 406), but, in terms of family inheritance, a pointedly more successful one.

The characters are presented as if they themselves are products of the earth. The Fouans are as if bound to the soil by the framing of their lives within the vast natural setting of the Beauce and the cyclical processes of Nature, in a broad compositional pattern governed by the rhythm of the seasons. Their relationship to the land is visceral, fluctuating according to the weather and the state of the crops. Sex and the language of sex—sowing, copulation, impregnation, procreation, fertility, harvesting—are everywhere, recurring as constants in the pattern of the narrative. Earth and body blend into each other: '[Lise] stretched out her great fat belly under the blazing sky so that it looked like a big seed sticking up in the fertile earth' (p. 200). The graphic description of the birth of her baby is juxtaposed with that of the calving of the family cow, both births taking place under the same roof. Fouan's body, after a lifetime of toil, has become shrivelled, and his stoop more pronounced, 'as if the earth was calling him' (p. 171). And when he actually is in the earth, in his coffin, Jean, standing at the graveside, looks down at the yellow pine box and is reminded of ripe wheat:

> in the dirt, he could make out the coffin, looking even smaller with
> its narrow pine lid the colour of golden wheat; and the lumps of the
> rich earth were sliding down, half covering the coffin so that he

could only see a pale patch of it at the bottom, like a handful of the seed which his comrades were casting into the furrows out on the plain.   (p. 423)

The fusion of body and earth assumes a particular, pervasive form: excrement, omnipresent image of fertility. Before the winter ploughing begins, the Beauce lies covered in manure as far as the eye can see:

On all sides the fields were covered with little heaps, a sort of heaving, surging sea of manure from cowshed and stable; while in some of them the piles had recently been spread out and the soil could be seen from afar stained with the dark, streaming tide of dung.
(p. 331)

Françoise, standing in a cart-load of manure, 'seemed very tall, strong and healthy, as if she had been growing in the manure and it was her own body that was giving off this rich, fertile smell' (p. 342). And there is 'Old Mother Poo', Frimat's wife, who uses human as well as animal excrement to nurture lush produce which she disposes of at the markets, her vegetables spurned by the locals but outgrowing and outselling those grown by more traditional methods. Her example has converted Hourdequin, who dreams of deploying the sewage of Paris to fertilize all the wheatfields of the Beauce. As Lise gives birth, the vet who has just delivered the calf bursts into the bedroom holding the animal in his arms, stark naked except for an apron, his entire body covered in dung. This provokes uncontrollable hilarity in Lise and her helpers, as the baby shoots out like a human cannon-ball: 'Cries at one end, laughter at the other' (p. 217).

Grotesque realism

As David Baguley notes, the scatological elements that pervade the text, far from reflecting a personal penchant for obscenity, belong to a literary tradition which the influential Russian literary critic Mikhail Bakhtin, in a celebrated study of the work of François Rabelais (1494–1553), calls 'grotesque realism'. This form of realism, rooted in the festive ('carnivalesque') spirit of popular culture of the Middle Ages, celebrates bodily life, in opposition to the harshness and drabness of everyday existence.

> …all that is bodily becomes grandiose, exaggerated, immeasurable…The leading themes of these images of bodily life are fertility, growth, and a brimming-over abundance…The essential principle of grotesque realism is degradation, that is, the lowering of all that is high, spiritual, ideal, abstract; it…relates to acts of defecation and copulation, conception, pregnancy, and birth. Degradation digs a bodily grave for a new birth; it has not only a destructive, negative aspect, but also a regenerating one.

The grape-harvest (part IV, chapter 4), with its Bacchanalian overtones, is emblematic of the festive principle in collective terms:

> a good week of tippling, in which disunited families usually reconciled around jugs of new wine. Rognes reeked of grapes for seven days; people ate so many the women would hitch up their skirts and the men drop their pants under every hedge…It wound up with drunken men and pregnant girls.   (p. 277)

The individual embodiment of the festive spirit is Jesus Christ. Dissolute, lazy, and wasteful, he is, as his blasphemous nickname suggests, irreverence incarnate. He tirelessly indulges the pleasures of the body, and often in a carnivalesque manner reflected most vividly in his virtuosity as a performer of farts. Nothing delights him more than the laughter and wonder he is able to engender by his feats of flatulence ('It was making him famous', p. 261), or his particular ability to show his dislike of priests. As the grape-pickers trudge home, the Abbé Madeline exchanging 'pious remarks' with a prostitute he mistakes for a lady, 'behind them came Jesus Christ, who was fiercely set against the man of the cloth and so started his disgusting stunt again, with the relentlessness of the true boozer' (p. 291). No wonder Jesus Christ feels brotherly admiration for that other embodiment of carnivalesque extravagance: the donkey Gideon, 'a practical joker, full of mischief' (p. 102), who, in an episode that closes the grape-picking chapter, creates 'an indecent spectacle' by drinking an entire tub of wine: 'dazed, losing all respect, he positively sneered and nodded his noggin to express unrepentant pleasure at his debauchery' (p. 293). Jesus Christ plays the Fool to Fouan's Lear. He is the clown who tells the truth: 'When you're in the ground eating dirt with the moles, a fat lot of good it'll have done you to have gone short now!' (p. 261). Who, indeed, is the real fool? Fouan's sister, La Grande, leaves her brother in no doubt when he talks to her about his decision to divide his property: 'You're a fool!' (p. 28). The scatological merriment of Jesus Christ is a burlesque expression of the poetry—the never-ending, regenerative fertility—of the Earth as Zola wished to evoke it.

The novel comes full circle, closing as it opens, with the sowing of seeds: an image of eternal renewal (Figure 11):

> In every direction, all over the rich clods of soil, men could be seen moving along with a steady sweep of their arms as they sowed. Jean could clearly see the golden seed, like a living cloud slipping from the hands of the nearest sowers. Then, as they became smaller and were lost in the infinite expanse, the seed swirled around them until, in the far distance, it seemed like the shimmering of the light itself.
>
> (p. 415)

As Jean stands in the graveyard behind the church, where Fouan is being buried, he witnesses the outbreak of a noisy, recurrent squabble over the position of the burial plots: 'peasants who have been at loggerheads in their lifetime don't like the idea of lying side by side when they are dead' (p. 418). Soon they are all shouting at once, fighting with each other, as they always have, amid the tombstones. But as Jean walks away, leaving Rognes for

11. Jean-François Millet, *The Sower*, 1850.

the last time, the outlook presented through the confused
thoughts swirling in his mind is that of Darwinian evolution. Even
the petty disputes, crimes, and violence perpetrated by human
beings, it is suggested, may play their part in the evolutionary
process, humanity shrinking to relative insignificance, like so
many tiny insects, within the great scheme of Nature and its
eternal laws.

Chapter 9
After the *Rougon-Macquart*

The later volumes of *Les Rougon-Macquart* reveal the increasing prominence of mythic discourse in the representation of social reality. Just as Zola situates man within a total context of shaping influences, so he tends more and more to relate the personal and social action of his novels to a synthesizing worldview. Jean's perspective at the end of *Earth* persists: life is a struggle between the forces of life and death, creation and destruction, degeneration and renewal. In *Money* (1891) and *La Débâcle* (1892), the eighteenth and nineteenth novels of the Rougon-Macquart series, heightened emphasis is given to the pattern of Eternal Return visible throughout Zola's work, from the cemetery bursting with fecund life in *The Fortune of the Rougons* to the climactic images of germination in *Germinal* and *Earth*.

An end and a new beginning

La Débâcle, which depicts the dramatic events of the Franco-Prussian War of 1870 and the Commune of 1871, brings to a close the history of the Second Empire. *Doctor Pascal* (1893) concludes the saga of the Rougon-Macquart family. Set in Plassans, the novel begins in 1872, after the fall of the Empire. Pascal Rougon, a doctor, first appears in *The Fortune of the Rougons* as the second son of Pierre and Félicité Rougon; his elder brother is Eugène Rougon, his younger brother is Aristide (Saccard). He stands apart, to such an extent that he does not seem to belong to the family at all. When he reappears twenty-two years later as the central figure of the novel that bears his name, it is as a heroic, almost messianic old man, a kind of scientist-scholar, prophesying a glorious future. Dedicated to medical research, he has spent his life studying genetics, chronicling and classifying the hereditary ills of his own family—the thirty descendants of his grandmother Adélaïde Fouque (Tante Dide). He keeps his files locked in a cupboard, along with a family tree he has painstakingly compiled. His young niece Clotilde, daughter of Aristide, has acquired strong religious convictions under the influence of Martine, the doctor's pious old servant. She considers her uncle's work a vain, even sacrilegious, attempt to understand what can be known only by God, and begs him to destroy his manuscripts. The conflict between science and religious faith is the focus of the first half of the novel. Pascal shows his niece the genealogical tree, and, one by one, reads out his files and comments on them, rehearsing in a single sitting the narratives Zola took twenty years to produce. Clotilde is won over, persuaded of the power of medical science and natural evolution.

Eventually, the doctor and his pupil begin an intimate and tender relationship, albeit incestuous. A financial crisis and burgeoning debts induce Pascal to send Clotilde away to Paris. He falls ill and dies before she can return. Félicité, desperate to keep the family skeletons hidden at any cost, burns her son's papers. Clotilde, on her return, finds fragments of his work, as well as the family tree, and resolves to complete the project. Her and Pascal's child is born several months later, and the novel closes in semi-idyllic fashion by focusing on the hope for the future, and for the regeneration of the family, which is symbolized by the child.

Zola expresses through Pascal what he called in his planning notes 'the whole philosophical meaning' of *Les Rougon-Macquart*: that is, his optimism. In *Doctor Pascal*, he is intent above all on responding to those who saw in *Les Rougon-Macquart*, with its chronicles of greed, corruption, and hereditary abnormality, nothing but morbidity and darkness. Zola also makes Pascal his double by turning him into an image (and symbolic affirmation) of himself as novelist. Pascal the fictional character is a surrogate of Zola the naturalist writer. The idea of Pascal as an author, rather than a simple participant—one more pathological 'case'—in the narrative of the Rougon-Macquart family, is reinforced by the fact, as he explains to Clotilde, that he is free of the family's inherited characteristics by virtue of his 'innateness' (the term used in biology to describe the process whereby some individuals are totally unaffected by the hereditary transmission of genetic characteristics). He is able to stand outside the world of his family, like an author in relation to the world of his characters. The effect of the novel's metafictional dimension—Pascal's outlining of the various narratives that make up the preceding nineteen novels of the Rougon-Macquart series, and his provision of supplementary details concerning the various family members—is to create in the reader an awareness that *Doctor Pascal*, and Zola's work generally, is not merely a defence of scientific materialism (and, in those terms, a defence of the naturalist project), nor simply a summarizing conclusion to *Les Rougon-Macquart*, but a *narrative* construction, an *imaginative* work.

The Pascal–Zola equation also has a deeply personal dimension, to which the myth of regenerative optimism is central. By the time Zola wrote *Doctor Pascal*, he had taken a mistress, Jeanne Rozerot, who had borne him two children, Denise in September 1889 and Jacques in September 1891. The official, printed dedication of *Le Docteur Pascal* reads: 'To the memory of MY MOTHER and to MY DEAR WIFE I dedicate this novel which is the summary and conclusion of my entire work.' On 23 June 1893 Zola gave a copy of the novel to Jeanne, and on the cover he had written:

> To my beloved Jeanne, to my Clotilde, who has given me the royal feast of her youth and taken thirty years off my life by giving me the

present of my Denise and my Jacques, the two dear children for whom I wrote this book, so that they might know, when they read it, how much I loved their mother and how tenderly they should repay her for the happiness with which she consoled me in my great sorrows.

Powerful currents of feeling flow through the portrayal in *Doctor Pascal* of the relationship between Pascal–Zola and Clotilde–Jeanne: pure happiness; deep mutual affection; a feeling of rejuvenation; the joy of erotic gratification, described lyrically and at length; the expression of 'forbidden love' in the casting of the lovers as uncle and niece; but also a fear of ageing, a melancholic sense of the irremediable distance in age, and a growing awareness, as in *The Bright Side of Life* (*La Joie de vivre*, 1884) but in a different register, of death's shadow—a personal dimension that gives great poignancy to Pascal's statement of belief in 'the ultimate triumph of life'. Pascal dies on the very day he receives word from Clotilde that she is pregnant; and the novel's conclusion celebrates a new life, Clotilde happily nursing their newborn son.

> The child had come, perhaps the redeemer…[s]he, his mother, was already dreaming of the future. What would he be, when she had made him big and strong by giving herself entirely? A scholar who would teach the world a bit of the eternal truth? A captain who would bring his country glory? Or, better still, one of those shepherds of men who quell passions and establish the reign of justice?

The child is the social messiah whose destiny will be traced in the novels Zola was yet to write. Zola's novels after *Les Rougon-Macquart* were inspired by his desire to respond, as he had begun to do in *Doctor Pascal*, to the changing intellectual climate of the period we call the *fin de siècle* (that is, roughly, the years between 1880 and 1900)—to engage polemically with contemporary debates about science and religion, and to consider the pressures placed on the democratic institutions of the Third Republic by social and political unrest.

The revolt against positivism

Much of the significant creative and discursive writing of the *fin de siècle* reflects the ideological strains of the period and, more narrowly, a powerful current of idealism: a sustained reaction against positivism and its claim that human reason could, through 'scientific method', come to know and understand everything. It became fashionable to speak of the 'bankruptcy' of science. The first collective manifestation of anti-positivist culture was the Decadent movement, which burst onto the French scene in 1884 with the publication of *Against Nature* (*A rebours*) by Joris-Karl Huysmans (1848–1907), and which was to become the dominant aesthetic of the *fin de siècle*. Huysmans began as a disciple of Zola, writing naturalist fiction (*Marthe*, 1876; *Married Life/En ménage*, 1881). *Against Nature* marked a deliberate break with naturalism and its materialist vision. The novel's anti-hero, a neurotic aristocrat named Des Esseintes, seeks to escape from the crass materialism of modern society by turning his back on it and withdrawing into a world of his own making. He dedicates himself to realizing his own private fantasies, attempting to create for himself an artificial paradise by living life 'back to front' or 'against nature', carrying to the point of psychopathology the vision of Charles Baudelaire, who initiated the Decadent obsession with the artificial and the perverse, arguing that the aim of literature and art was not to imitate nature but to negate it.

Zola's naturalism began to be explicitly rejected by erstwhile admirers. In 1886 Count Eugène-Melchior de Vogüé published a study of the Russian novel, in which he made a famous plea for a novel free from the shackles of naturalism, a novel which would deal with matters of the spirit as well as the flesh. There was a remarkable revival of Catholic literature and a spate of conversions to Catholicism among the literary elite. Notable examples of these conversions were Huysmans, Léon Bloy (1846–1917), Paul Bourget (1852–1935), and Paul Claudel

(1868–1955). In his novel *The Disciple* (*Le Disciple*, 1889) Bourget, a former disciple of Taine, proclaimed the emptiness of positivist doctrines and the dangers of a life unsupported by absolute moral values. Positivism was further undermined by the writings of the philosopher Henri Bergson (1859–1941), who, in his *Time and Free Will* (*Essai sur les données immédiates de la conscience*, 1889) and his public lectures at the Collège de France, stressed the existence within people of intuitive forces totally at odds with the mechanistic view of human behaviour embodied in positivism.

During this period there was, also, a growing mood of pessimism concerning the well-being of the nation. The psychological impact of France's defeat at the hands of the Prussians in 1870 should not be underestimated; nor indeed should the fears caused by the nation's declining birth rate. Moral critics blamed the military disaster at Sedan on demographic decline and moral degeneracy, while writers like the social psychologist Gustave Le Bon (1841–1931) began to develop theories of racial-historical decline, displacing the notion of degeneration from individual degenerates (cretins, criminals, the insane) to society (crowds, masses, cities). In a sense, degeneration theory was the dark side of Darwinian evolutionary theories of progress. Evolution, it was claimed, proceeds unevenly, and at any moment there are forces that pull us back down the evolutionary ladder.

Three Cities

The novel trilogy *Three Cities*, consisting of *Lourdes* (1894), *Rome* (1896), and *Paris* (1898), follows the life of a young priest, Pierre Froment, who progressively loses his faith. These novels treat in a sustained manner the anti-clericalism and anti-Catholicism embodied in priests throughout *Les Rougon-Macquart*: the priest who counsels Lisa in *The Belly of Paris*; the ruthless Faujas, agent of the Bonapartist regime in *The Conquest of Plassans*; the hysterical Serge Mouret in *The Sin of Abbé Mouret*; the ineffectual Abbé Mauduit in *Pot Luck*, sweeping under the carpet the adulteries of his bourgeois parishioners; the insensitive Abbé Ranvier in *Germinal*; the brutal bishop Monseigneur Hautecoeur in *The Dream*.

The revival of faith in France (and the revival of Catholicism generally) owed much to a 14-year-old peasant girl, Bernadette Soubirous, who, in 1858, near the village of Lourdes in the foothills of the Pyrenees, claimed to have seen the Virgin Mary in a grotto. The grotto became a shrine. A basilica was erected. Annual mass pilgrimages were instituted. Thousands flocked to Lourdes to bathe in water from a spring Bernadette had found, to gain relief or a cure for one illness or another. Pierre joins one such pilgrimage. He doubts the authenticity of the 'supernatural' cures, feeling that they have much to do with hysteria and the power of suggestion; and during his stay he observes how the Church has turned the pilgrimages into a commercial industry. In September 1894, not only *Lourdes* but the entirety of Zola's work was placed on the Vatican's Index of prohibited books.

On the basis of his experiences in the Paris slums, Pierre has written a book advocating a system of Christian socialism. To defend his book against the threat of being placed on the Index, he travels to Rome. In contrast to his ultraconservative predecessor, Pius IX, whose encyclical of 1864, *Quanta Cura*, represented a blanket denunciation of modernity, Pope Leo XIII preached reconciliation with the anti-clerical French Republic. In *Rerum Novarum*, the encyclical of 1891 that earned him the title of 'the workers' pope', he enjoined Catholics to find a means of regulating the excesses of capitalism by social activism. However, despite the pope's avowed liberalism, Pierre finds the Church conservative and corrupt, and the papacy ossified by dogma and obsessed with intrigue.

He returns to Paris and finds the city shaken by anarchist bombings and shocked by the Panama scandal of 1892 (when French government ministers took bribes to keep quiet about the financial troubles of the Panama Canal Company). At the same time, anti-Semitism is rife and anti-parliamentary nationalism on the rise. Sceptical of the power of faith, and having lost hope for the renewal of Catholicism, Pierre now tests the limits of charity. He soon concludes that what for centuries has passed for Christian charity—the forever rich giving alms to the forever poor—is totally inadequate to the deepening social problems of the modern world. Gradually his Catholicism is replaced by belief in science, which will become the great motor of social progress, justice, and harmony in the France of the future. *Paris* was published in March 1898, but its appearance was overshadowed by the accelerating drama of the Dreyfus Affair.

The Dreyfus Affair

Zola's fiction, together with his voluminous, often polemical journalistic writings, is broadly definable in terms of his engagement with public affairs. It was entirely logical that in 1898 he crowned his literary career with a political act, 'J'accuse!', his famous open letter to the President of the Republic, Félix Faure, in defence of Alfred Dreyfus. 'The Affair' (as it came to be called) was of momentous significance in modern French history. It split the political class and polarized public opinion, not simply on the particular question of Dreyfus's innocence or guilt but on the nation's identity. It magnified the fault-lines of the Third Republic and its major institutions, reflecting the profound differences between the revolutionary and counter-revolutionary traditions in France.

The Affair began in September 1894, when a cleaning lady in the German Embassy retrieved from the waste-paper basket of the military attaché, Colonel von Schwartzkoppen, an unsigned memorandum in French. The memorandum suggested that classified information about French armaments had been passed to the Germans. The cleaner was in the pay of the intelligence service (the wonderfully named 'Statistics Section') of the French War Ministry, and the memorandum, which would become known as the *bordereau*, soon reached the War Minister, General Mercier. The military establishment was baffled, but needed a scapegoat. It was desperate to protect its reputation following its humiliating defeat in 1870. Nationalist feeling was very strong; there were fears of aggression by a newly united Germany; and there was a wave of anti-Semitism on a scale not to be matched in Europe until Hitler's rise to power in the 1930s. Édouard Drumont's anti-Semitic tract *La France juive* sold over a million copies during the twenty-five years following its publication in 1886.

The attention of the military establishment turned to Dreyfus, who was a member of a wealthy family of textile manufacturers in German-speaking Alsace, and the first Jew to have succeeded in becoming a staff officer. Meritocratic reform had drawn into the army outsiders like Dreyfus, but this also made him the object of suspicion by the old Catholic families, who traditionally manned France's officer class. On the basis of a vague similarity between his handwriting and that on the *bordereau*, he was arrested. The court-martial took place in private, at the request of the prosecution. One of the senior officers of the intelligence service, Major Henry, declared under oath that a 'man of substance' had warned them that a traitor was at work in the War Ministry. He pointed to Dreyfus. When, on 22 December, the military judges retired to consider their verdict, they were shown a 'secret dossier'—in fact, false evidence concocted by Henry. Dreyfus was convicted of treason and sentenced to deportation for life. In April 1895, he was settled in solitary confinement on Devil's Island.

Dreyfus was largely forgotten. But in March 1896, Schwartzkoppen's waste-paper basket produced another document, this time a *petit bleu*, one of the blue letter-cards used for express delivery within Paris. The card was addressed to a French officer named Esterhazy. Esterhazy was known to be dissolute and to have a gambling problem, but he was the son of a distinguished general. The *petit bleu* was passed to Lieutenant-Colonel Georges Picquart, the new head of the intelligence service.

In August 1896, Picquart was able to view samples of Esterhazy's handwriting, and saw immediately that it was the same as that on the *bordereau*. Soon afterwards, he gained access to the secret dossier shown to the judges in 1894, which had been stored in Henry's safe. The dossier contained nothing that applied, directly or indirectly, to Dreyfus. Picquart drew up a report, accusing Esterhazy of the treason. His superiors decided that they must get him out of the way. In January 1897 he was packed off, on regimental duty, to Tunisia, where it was hoped he would be killed. Meanwhile the new War Minister, General Billot, informed the Chamber of Deputies that High Command had come into possession of evidence (a document forged, once more, by Henry) that established Dreyfus's guilt beyond doubt. On 4 December 1897 the Chamber voted to affirm the verdict of the 1894 court-martial, and Prime Minister Méline announced 'There is no Dreyfus Affair'. Meanwhile, Dreyfus's brother Mathieu had publicly denounced Esterhazy, who was advised to request a court-martial: given the attitude of the military establishment, he would surely be acquitted.

At the time of Dreyfus's arrest, Zola had been in Rome, engaged in preparatory work for his novel set in the Italian capital. On 16 May 1896, he had published an article in *Le Figaro* entitled 'A Plea for the Jews' ('Pour les juifs'), denouncing the anti-Semitism that appeared endemic in the France of the 1880s and 1890s; but he made no mention of Dreyfus. Like many others at the time, he took it for granted that Dreyfus was guilty. However, towards the end of 1896, as a result of representations by campaigners for Dreyfus, he became convinced not only that Dreyfus was innocent but that he, Zola, had to do something. In any consideration of the reasons for this decision, his personal background must be borne in mind. As a child he had experienced something akin to racism; in Aix he was mocked by his schoolmates as an outsider (indeed, a foreigner), and when he returned to Paris the same thing happened again. The fact that his father was not French would be used to denigrate him at the height of the Affair. He wrote a series of articles in *Le Figaro*, and two pamphlets: *Letter to the Young Men of France* (*Lettre à la jeunesse*) and *Letter to France* (*Lettre à la France*). Though written with passion and skill, they made little impression on public opinion. However, Zola had conceived a bold strategy that would take the case out of the military courts and put it before the civil courts and the public.

The Esterhazy court-martial opened on 10 January 1898. The various witnesses were heard in private. A new team of handwriting experts dutifully swore that Esterhazy had not written the *bordereau*, and, farcically, he was acquitted on 11 January. Immediately, Zola told Ernest Vaughan and Georges Clemenceau, the co-editors of the new left-wing newspaper *L'Aurore*, to expect an article the following morning. 'J'accuse!' covered the whole front page on 13 January 1898. After listing the judicial errors, the manipulation of evidence, and the flouting of legal procedure, Zola denounced the high-level corruption surrounding Esterhazy's trial. At the end of his letter, he made it clear that his accusations, including the naming of some of the senior officers behind the conspiracy against Dreyfus, were meant to be self-incriminating in terms of the current libel laws.

'J'accuse!' burst on the public with enormous force (Figure 12). Three hundred thousand copies of *L'Aurore* were sold in the streets—ten times the newspaper's normal circulation. The article relaunched the Dreyfusard movement and turned Zola into one of the main protagonists in the Affair. He received thousands of letters of support, and a number of death threats. A series of petitions calling for a judicial review of the Dreyfus case were signed by leading writers and artists—Léon Blum, Anatole France, Octave Mirbeau, Charles Péguy, Marcel Proust, and many others. Billot denounced in the Chamber the 'anti-patriotic attacks' that were damaging the army's reputation. Anti-Semitic demonstrations took place in the Latin Quarter, and anti-Jewish riots broke out in many towns throughout France. The Affair now reached fever-pitch. Zola was portrayed as the front man of a

12. A contemporary cartoon. With his pen, Zola attacks the army personnel whom, in his newspaper article 'J'accuse!', he accused of corruption and knowingly convicting an innocent man. On Zola's side are the intellectuals and Dreyfusards.

German-Jewish plot. He was ruthlessly vilified in the right-wing press. The new Roman Catholic newspaper *La Croix* played a prominent role in the campaign. Zola's assailants did their best to link the 'corrupting' and 'demoralizing' influence of his novels with the 'unpatriotic' nature of his intervention in the Affair; as he had besmirched proper standards of good taste in literature, so now, they said, he was besmirching the honour of France. Caricaturists constantly targeted his alleged obsession with lavatories, filth, and faecal matter. It was from the time of the Affair that a chamber-pot came to be known in many households as 'a zola'. One cartoon depicted him as a pig defecating on the French flag. Maurice Barrès whipped up racist slurs: 'the man is not French…Émile Zola naturally thinks like a deracinated Venetian.'

Billot and Méline promised in the Chamber of Deputies that Zola would be prosecuted for defamation of the army. This was precisely what Zola wanted. The trial opened at the Palais de Justice on 7 February. It was covered by journalists from around the world. Zola was greeted on his arrival by crowds yelling abuse. The presiding judge cut off debate each time the defence strayed from the Esterhazy case, but the military were provoked into alluding inadvertently to the 'secret dossier' and the document subsequently forged by Henry. Also, Zola's lawyer, Fernand Labori, called expert witnesses who all testified that the handwriting of the *bordereau* was Esterhazy's. The result, however, was a foregone conclusion. On 23 February, Zola was found guilty and given the maximum sentence of twelve months in prison and a fine of 3,000 francs. On 2 April, his appeal was upheld on a technicality, but on 18 July the sentence was confirmed. Labori and Clemenceau persuaded Zola to leave the country immediately, not so much to avoid imprisonment but because they felt that this would be better for Dreyfus's cause. He left for England by the evening boat-train.

On 13 August the War Minister's aide, a Captain Cuignet, discovered that one of the documents concocted by Henry was a blatant forgery. On 30 August Henry was interviewed. He confessed, was arrested, and imprisoned, whereupon he slit his throat with a razor. Esterhazy fled to Belgium, and then to England, where he admitted that he had written the *bordereau*. On 3 June 1899 the 1894 judgement on Dreyfus was quashed and a second trial by court-martial ordered. Zola returned immediately to Paris. Dreyfus was brought back from Devil's Island. The retrial was conducted for security reasons outside Paris, in Rennes. On 9 September the court again found Dreyfus guilty, 'with extenuating circumstances' (these circumstances were not specified, of course). When this second guilty verdict made it clear that no court-martial would admit to a miscarriage of justice, a presidential pardon was issued, which Dreyfus, on the urging of his family but to the dismay of his supporters, accepted. Formal exoneration came, by act of parliament, in 1906, four years after Zola's death.

The significance of the Dreyfus Affair for French society was enormous. It produced a rallying of support for the democratic institutions of the Republic against its royalist, Catholic, and authoritarian opponents (though it also led to the creation of Charles Maurras's anti-republican, nationalist movement, the Action Française, which remained an influential group during the first forty years of the 20th century until it ceased to exist because of its association with the collaborationist Vichy government of 1940–4). In July 1901 a new law compelled religious congregations to apply for legal authorization or be dissolved, and no member of an unauthorized congregation was to be allowed to teach; and in 1905 the Church was formally separated from the state.

One of the chief legacies of the Affair was the birth of the modern notion of the intellectual. It was in the context of the petitions of January 1898 that the noun *intellectuel* became popularized. In broad terms, an intellectual, whether of the left or right, was understood to be a writer or thinker whose duty was to engage with his or her age, who defended a position with reference to a set of general principles or an ideology, and was prepared to enter the public arena to argue his or her case. Writers like Maurice Barrès, who became Zola's chief antagonist, invoked their belief in the institutions that enshrined national traditions, such as the Church and the army; Zola and others, as liberal intellectuals, affirmed their commitment to the principles underpinning the revolution of 1789—principles which, they believed, should transcend national self-interest. During his second trial Zola declared to the jury:

> There is only one issue. Is France still the France of the Revolution and the Declaration of the Rights of Man, the France which gave the world liberty, and was supposed to give it justice?

Zola's courageous stand over the Dreyfus Affair showed the 'public writer' at his best—squarely in the tradition of Voltaire and Victor Hugo, and anticipating the 'committed' generation of Jean-Paul Sartre and Albert Camus.

Utopia

Under the impulse, no doubt, of the profound social crisis
embodied in the Affair, Zola had embarked on a new cycle of
novels, *The Four Gospels* (*Les Quatre Évangiles*), setting out a
utopian vision for a new France. Pierre Froment, the hero of *Three
Cities*, fathers four sons, each of whom is destined to be the hero
of a Gospel. As with *Three Cities*, *The Four Gospels* raised the
possibility of a secularized replacement for Christianity in an
age of reason and progress. These works provide insights into
the preoccupations and hopes of French people as the 19th
century turned into the 20th, but they lack imaginative
conviction. Tracts rather than novels, their prolixity provoked
Henry James into remarking acidly that in them 'everything is
absent but quantity'.

Quantity is the very subject of *Fecundity* (*Fécondité*, 1899), which
was written in the context of public debate concerning France's
declining birth rate. The novel is a hymn to procreation and a
polemic against birth control and abortion. Mathieu Froment and
his wife Marianne beget a family that grows exponentially. Zola's
belief in indefinite future progress built on technical innovations
and scientific discoveries made him confident that an increasing
population would not lead to food shortages or economic
hardship. Moreover, the Froments' fecundity opens up new vistas
for humanity as a whole, for their descendants found and populate
a new colony in Africa, bringing enlightenment and progress in
their wake.

Work (*Travail*, 1901) describes Luc Froment's creation of an ideal
society. Work is equated with fecundity, which becomes both a
moral imperative and a principle of social organization. The basis
of Luc's utopian community, La Crècherie, is man's creative energy,
the use of the human passions within a harmonious and rationally
organized society. The model was derived from the writings of the

early socialist thinker Charles Fourier (1772–1837). The idea of a harmonious city means greater efficiency in that Luc's rational exploitation of the passions entails the elimination of waste and the suppression of all non-productive, parasitic elements.

The lessons of bourgeois degeneracy in *Work* are that idleness is a sin, class exploitation is wasteful, and parasitism subverts the efficiency and humane organization of the working community. Zola suggests, however, that collective action by the workers offers no hope of social reform. He stresses the conservatism and inertia of the workers, who play a negligible part in the social transformation represented by La Crècherie; and his critique of their political apathy is matched by explicit disapproval of the collectivist and anarchist ideologies of revolutionary activists. Luc, on the other hand, is seen as a charismatic leader. The New Man who comes to redeem and rebuild is a bourgeois reformer whose prestige as the founder and benign ruler of the perfect city-state merely increases with the passing years. Zola's final vision of the ideal society corresponds to class collaboration and a rearranged bourgeois hierarchy. The propertied bourgeoisie of the exploitative, capitalist variety is eclipsed by a new managerial elite. The only character whose prestige is comparable to Luc's is Jordan, the gifted technocrat who embodies Zola's faith in science. Although the novel's point of departure is a crisis of industrial capitalism, the ideological basis of the social reforms advocated is not scientific socialism but a form of bourgeois paternalism. As Henri Mitterand has commented, *Work* 'reads like *Germinal* in reverse, like a fully peace-loving, harmonious, and quite patriarchal construction of a new city, with neither confrontations nor convulsions'.

Truth (*Vérité*), published posthumously in 1903, is a transposition of the Dreyfus Affair. Its hero is Marc Froment, a schoolteacher passionately devoted to truth and justice; he fights to defend a Jewish colleague wrongfully accused of having sexually abused and murdered his young nephew. The actual murderer is a monk, one of the boy's teachers at a school run by a Catholic order. The novel ends with a vision of a France—an enlightened, republican France—free of religious obscurantism and revitalized by the dynamic force of education; there is no occupation more noble than that of the primary schoolteacher, the *instituteur*, the embodiment of republican virtues, whose mission is to make of his pupils the happy citizens of the future.

Justice, which would depict universal peace in a supra-racial congress of nations, remained unwritten: death intervened.

Death

Zola died on 29 September 1902, in his Paris home, of carbon monoxide poisoning. Although the official police investigation concluded, on the basis of an autopsy, that Zola's death was an accident, various tests showed only tiny concentrations of carbon monoxide in the air, and an examination of the chimney flue failed to reveal any serious blockage. There has been much speculation that Zola was in fact murdered as an act of political revenge over his role in the Dreyfus Affair. It is impossible to overestimate the feelings of hatred that persisted after the quashing of the 1894 verdict on Dreyfus and the return of Zola to France, and for many years afterwards. The writer (and his wife) continued to receive abusive letters, some of which threatened violence. On 31 July 1901, a box containing a makeshift bomb had been discovered in the entrance to the apartment building in the Rue de Bruxelles. It was dismantled by the police.

In 1953 a young journalist, Jean Bedel, published a series of articles on Zola's death in the left-wing newspaper *Libération*, in which he described how a man named Pierre Hacquin, a retired chemist, had told him that in April 1927, while living in Sarcelles (in the northern suburbs of Paris), a friend of his, a former stove and chimney fitter, had confessed a few weeks before his death that, while working on the roof of the building which contained Zola's apartment at 21 *bis*, Rue de Bruxelles, he had blocked the chimney leading down to the novelist's bedroom, and unblocked it the next day. It was only in 1978, in the *Quotidien de Paris*, that Bedel revealed the name of the fitter: Henri Buronfosse. In their *Guide Emile Zola*, Alain Pagès and Owen Morgan describe their research into Buronfosse's life. They ascertained that he was indeed a stove and chimney fitter based in the fourth *arrondissement* of Paris, and that he died in Sarcelles in May 1928 (his confession must therefore have occurred in April of that year, not in April 1927). Most significantly, Pagès and Morgan demonstrate the plausibility of Buronfosse's having been a member, as Hacquin mentioned to Bedel, of the far-right Ligue des Patriotes (League of Patriots). Was Buronfosse's confession authentic? We cannot know for sure, but the body of evidence—not material evidence, but research and accumulated information—points to the probability of murder, whether intended or not. The police *commissaire* who led the inquiry into Zola's death told a journalist twenty years later, after his retirement, that he had suspected foul play, but had been unable to prove it; his inquiry had been carried out in summary fashion, for neither the state nor the Zola family wished to stir up the simmering animosities of the Dreyfus Affair.

More than 50,000 people, according to *L'Aurore*, accompanied Zola's coffin to Montmartre Cemetery on 5 October. The crowd included Alfred Dreyfus and a delegation of miners from Denain. Anatole France delivered a moving eulogy: Zola, he concluded, was 'a moment in the history of the human conscience'. On 3 June 1908, Zola's remains were transferred to the Panthéon. A crowd of several thousand protesters had to be forced back to allow the hearse to pass. Forty arrests were made. The next day, as the official ceremony of reburial drew to a close, two shots rang out, and it was realized that Dreyfus had been hit. Fortunately, he only suffered a flesh wound. His assailant was a journalist and ex-soldier named Louis Grégori, who felt that the army was being insulted by the consecration. He was arrested (and, after a perfunctory trial, acquitted of all charges). After a short delay, Zola's remains were placed in the crypt below. He was only the fourth French writer to be buried in the Panthéon, following Voltaire (1791), Rousseau (1794), and Victor Hugo (1885).

A chronology of Zola's life and works

(The novels that form part of the Rougon-Macquart series are indicated by an asterisk.)

1840   (2 April) Born in Paris, the only child of Francesco Zola (b. 1795), an Italian engineer, and Émilie Aubert (b. 1819), the daughter of a glazier. The naturalist novelist was later proud that 'zolla' in Italian means 'clod of earth'.

1843   Family moves to Aix-en-Provence, which will become the town of 'Plassans' in the Rougon-Macquart novels.

1847   (27 March) Death of father from pneumonia following a chill caught while supervising work on his scheme to supply Aix-en-Provence with drinking water. The family is left almost destitute.

1848   Starts school at the Pension Notre-Dame.

1851   (2 December) Coup d'état of Louis-Napoleon Bonaparte, president of the short-lived Second Republic (1848–51). Erection of barricades in Paris and Republican uprisings in the provinces (in Provence, for example, as described by Zola in *The Fortune of the Rougons*).

1852   (2 December) Louis-Napoleon proclaimed Emperor Napoleon III.

1852–8	Boarder at the Collège Bourbon (now the Collège Mignet). Friendship with the future painter Paul Cézanne.
1858	(February) Leaves Aix to join his mother in Paris (she had moved there in December). Offered a place and bursary at the Lycée Saint-Louis. (November) Falls ill with typhoid and convalescence is slow.
1859	Fails his *baccalauréat* twice.
1860	(Spring) Employed as a copy clerk in the Excise Office of the Paris docks, but abandons it after two months, preferring to eke out an existence as a writer in the Latin Quarter. A period of severe poverty. These years see the height of the urban redevelopment programme undertaken by Baron Haussmann, Prefect of the Seine from 1853 to 1869.
1862	(February) Taken on by Hachette, the well-known publishing house, at first in the dispatch office, then as head of the publicity department. (31 October) Naturalized as French citizen.
1863	(31 January) First literary article published. (1 May) Manet's *Le Déjeuner sur l'herbe* exhibited at the Salon des Refusés, which Zola visits with Cézanne.
1864	(October) Publishes *Tales for Ninon* (*Contes à Ninon*), a collection of short stories.
1865	Publishes first novel, *Claude's Confession* (*La Confession de Claude*). A *succès de scandale* thanks to its bedroom scenes. Meets future wife, Alexandrine-Gabrielle Meley (b. 1839).
1866	Leaves Hachette and becomes a literary critic on the recently launched daily *L'Événement*. Frequents the Café Guerbois in the Batignolles district of Paris, the meeting-place of the future Impressionist painters. Writes a series of provocative articles attacking the official Salon Selection Committee, and praising Manet and Monet. (July) Publishes *Mon Salon*. Summer months spent with Cézanne at Bennecourt on the Seine.

1867   (January) Publishes article on Manet, 'Une nouvelle manière en peinture: Édouard Manet' ('A New Way to Paint: Édouard Manet'). (December) Publication of *Thérèse Raquin*.

1868   (April) Preface to second edition of *Thérèse Raquin*: champions the literary ideology he terms 'naturalism'. (December) Publication of *Madeleine Férat*. Begins to plan the Rougon-Macquart series of novels.

1868–70   Continues working as journalist for various newspapers.

1870   (31 May) Marries Alexandrine. (September) Moves temporarily to Marseilles because of the Franco-Prussian War, declared on 19 July. Fall of the Second Empire. The Third Republic is declared. Paris is besieged by Prussian forces. Spends several months in Bordeaux, reporting on the deliberations of the provisional Government of National Defence.

1871   (March) Returns to Paris. Witnesses the civil war of the Commune and the carnage brought about by its fall. (October) Publishes *The Fortune of the Rougons* (*La Fortune des Rougon*)*, the first of the twenty novels making up the Rougon-Macquart series.

1872   Publication of *The Kill* (*La Curée*)*.

1873   Publication of *The Belly of Paris* (*Le Ventre de Paris*)*.

1874   (May) Publication of *The Conquest of Paris* (*La Conquête de Plassans*)*. (November) Publication of *Further Tales for Ninon* (*Nouveaux Contes à Ninon*).

1875   Begins to contribute articles to the Russian newspaper *Vestnik Evropy* (*The European Herald*). (April) Publication of *The Sin of Abbé Mouret* (*La Faute de l'abbé Mouret*)*.

1876   Publication of *His Excellency Eugène Rougon* (*Son Excellence Eugène Rougon*)*.

1877   (February) Publication of *L'Assommoir**. The novel is a bestseller. The Zolas move to a comfortable apartment at 23, Rue de Boulogne (now Rue Ballu). (April) Dinner held at Restaurant Trapp to inaugurate the 'naturalist school'.

1878	Buys a house at Médan on the Seine, 40 kilometres west of Paris. (June) Publication of *A Love Story* (*Une page d'amour*)*.
1880	(March) Publication of *Nana**, which attracts further scandal to Zola's name. (April) Publication of *Les Soirées de Médan* ('Evenings at Médan'), a collection of short stories by Zola and some of his naturalist 'disciples'. (8 May) Death of Gustave Flaubert. (17 October) Death of Zola's mother. Suffers from depression and psychosomatic illness. (December) Publication in volume form of *The Experimental Novel* (*Le Roman expérimental*), a collection of essays expounding the theory of naturalism.
1882	Publication of *Pot Luck* (*Pot-Bouille*)*.
1883	Publication of *The Ladies' Paradise* (*Au Bonheur des Dames*)*.
1884	Publication of *The Bright Side of Life* (*La Joie de vivre*)*.
1885	Publication of *Germinal**.
1886	Publication of *The Masterpiece* (*L'Œuvre*)*.
1887	Publication of *Earth* (*La Terre*)*. Denounced as an onanistic pornographer in the 'Manifesto of the Five' in *Le Figaro*.
1888	Publication of *The Dream* (*Le Rêve*)*. Beginning of lifelong relationship with Jeanne Rozerot, a seamstress employed by Madame Zola.
1889	(20 September) Birth of Denise, daughter of Zola and Jeanne. The Zolas move to 21*bis*, Rue de Bruxelles. Zola's candidature for the Académie française fails, as will his nineteen subsequent attempts to gain membership. Henry Vizetelly condemned to three months' imprisonment for publishing English translations of Zola's novels.
1890	Publication of *La Bête humaine**.
1891	Publication of *Money* (*L'Argent*)*. (April) Elected President of the Société des Gens de Lettres. (25 September) Birth of Jacques, son of Zola and Jeanne.
1892	Publication of *La Débâcle**.

1893	Publication of *Doctor Pascal* (*Le Docteur Pascal*)*, the last of the Rougon-Macquart novels. Visits London as the guest of the Institute of Journalists and attends a banquet in his honour at the Crystal Palace.
1894	Publication of *Lourdes*, the first novel of the trilogy *Three Cities* (*Les Trois Villes*). (22 December) Alfred Dreyfus, a Jewish army officer, convicted by court-martial of spying for Germany and sentenced to life imprisonment on Devil's Island.
1896	Publication of *Rome*.
1898	(13 January) 'J'accuse!', Zola's open letter in defence of Dreyfus, published in *L'Aurore*. (21 February) Found guilty of libelling the Minister of War and given the maximum sentence of one year's imprisonment and a fine of 3,000 francs. Appeal for retrial granted on a technicality. (March) Publication of *Paris*. (23 May) Retrial delayed. (18 July) Leaves for England instead of attending court.
1899	(4 June) The Dreyfus case is reopened and Zola returns to France. (October) Publication of *Fecundity* (*Fécondité*), the first of Zola's *Four Gospels* (*Les Quatre Évangiles*).
1901	Publication of *Work* (*Travail*), the second 'Gospel'.
1902	(29 September) Dies of carbon monoxide fumes from his bedroom fire, the chimney having been capped either by accident or by anti-Dreyfusard design. Alexandrine survives. (5 October) Public funeral at the Cimetière Montmartre, witnessed by a crowd of 50,000.
1903	*Truth* (*Vérité*), the third 'Gospel', published posthumously. *Justice* (*La Justice*) was to have been the fourth.
1908	(4 June) Remains transferred to the Panthéon.

References

Introduction

Anita Brookner, *The Genius of the Future: Studies in French Art Criticism* (London: Phaidon, 1971), p. 91.
A. Alvarez, *The Writer's Voice* (New York: W. W. Norton, 2005).

Chapter 1: Zola and the art of fiction

Henri Mitterand, 'De l'ethnographie à la fiction', in *Le Regard et le signe: poétique du roman réaliste et naturaliste* (Paris: PUF, 1987), pp. 75–91.
Chantal Pierre-Gnassounou, in Brian Nelson, ed., *The Cambridge Companion to Émile Zola* (Cambridge: Cambridge University Press, 2007), p. 100.
Susan Harrow, *Zola, The Body Modern: Pressures and Prospects of Representation* (London: Legenda, 2010).

Chapter 2: Before the *Rougon-Macquart*

'A New Way to Paint: Édouard Manet' is included in Émile Zola, *Looking at Manet*, with an introduction by Robert Lethbridge (London: Pallas Athene, 2013).
'the open-air dance hall…': Henri Mitterand, *Émile Zola: Fiction and Modernity*, trans. and ed. Monica Lebron and David Baguley (London: The Émile Zola Society, 2000), p. 144.

'In *Thérèse Raquin* I set out…': Émile Zola, *Thérèse Raquin*, trans. and ed. Andrew Rothwell (Oxford: Oxford University Press, 1992), p. 1. Subsequent page references are included in the text.

Linda Nochlin, *Realism* (Harmondsworth: Penguin Books, 1971), p. 41.

Chapter 3: The fat and the thin: *The Belly of Paris*

Quotations from the novel are taken from Émile Zola, *The Belly of Paris*, trans. and ed. Brian Nelson (Oxford: Oxford University Press, 2007).

'the story of Cain and Abel…': Naomi Schor, *Zola's Crowds* (Baltimore: Johns Hopkins University Press, 1978), p. 27.

Chapter 4: 'A work of truth': *L'Assommoir*

Quotations from the novel have been translated by Brian Nelson.

'The Parisian bourgeoisie…': Philip Walker, *Zola* (London: Routledge & Kegan Paul, 1985), p. 123.

'De la description', *Le Voltaire*, 8 June 1880; included in *Le Roman expérimental*.

'human dignity…': Valerie Minogue, *Zola: 'L'Assommoir'* (London: Grant & Cutler, 1991), p. 14; see also pp. 87–8 and 91–3.

Henry James, *Literary Criticism: French Writers, Other European Writers, The Prefaces to the New York Edition*, ed. Leon Edel (New York: Library of America, 1984), pp. 892–3.

Chapter 5: The man-eater: *Nana*

Quotations from the novel are taken from Émile Zola, *Nana*, trans. Helen Constantine, ed. Brian Nelson (Oxford: Oxford University Press, 2020).

Virginia Rounding, *Grandes Horizontales* (London: Bloomsbury, 2003), pp. 3–4. The major theme of David Baguley's excellent study of Napoleon III, *Napoleon III and his Regime: An Extavaganza* (Baton Rouge: Louisiana State University Press, 2000), is the Emperor's assiduous manufacture of his public image.

'The *demi-monde*…': Virginia Rounding, *Grandes Horizontales*, p. 2.

Ilona Chessid, *Thresholds of Desire: Authority and Transgression in the* Rougon-Macquart (New York: Peter Lang, 1993), p. 71.

'a theatre run amok': Ilona Chessid, *Thresholds of Desire*, p. 71.

David Baguley, 'Zola, the Novelist(s)', in Robert Lethbridge and Terry Keefe, eds, *Zola and the Craft of Fiction* (Leicester: Leicester University Press, 1990), pp. 15–27 (p. 22).

Gustave Flaubert, letter to Zola, 15 Feb. 1880.

Peter Brooks, *Realist Vision* (New Haven and London: Yale University Press, 2005), p. 119.

Nana's sexuality…: see Peter Brooks, *Realist Vision*, chapter 7: 'Zola's Combustion Chamber', pp. 113–29.

Roland Barthes, 'The Man-Eater', in David Baguley, ed., *Critical Essays on Emile Zola* (Boston: G. K. Hall, 1986), pp. 90–3 (p. 90).

Bill Overton, *Fictions of Female Adultery, 1684–1890: Theories and Circumtexts* (London: Palgrave Macmillan, 2002), p. 171.

Chapter 6: The dream machine: *The Ladies' Paradise*

Quotations from the novel are taken from Émile Zola, *The Ladies' Paradise*, trans. and ed. Brian Nelson (Oxford: Oxford University Press, 1995).

'the poem of modern-day activity…': quoted by Henri Mitterand in Émile Zola, *Les Rougon-Macquart*, vol. 3 (Paris: Gallimard, Bibliothèque de la Pléiade, 1964), p. 1679.

The Bon Marché: see Michael Miller, *The Bon Marché: Bourgeois Culture and the Department Store, 1869–1920* (Princeton: Princeton University Press, 1981).

'Their theatricality…': David Harvey, *Paris, Capital of Modernity* (New York & London: Routledge, 2003), p. 216.

'In the Bon Marché vision…': Michael Miller, *The Bon Marché*, p. 227.

Chapter 7: Down the mine: *Germinal*

Quotations from the novel have been translated by Brian Nelson.

'At the risk…': quoted by Frederick Brown in *Zola: A Life* (New York: Farrar, Straus, Giroux, 1995), pp. 544–5.

Chapter 8: The Great Mother: *Earth*

Quotations from the novel are taken from Émile Zola, *Earth*, trans. Brian Nelson and Julie Rose, ed. Brian Nelson (Oxford: Oxford University Press, 2016).

David Baguley, *Naturalist Fiction: The Entropic Vision* (Cambridge: Cambridge University Press, 1990), p. 160.

The 'Manifesto of the Five' has been published in English translation
in David Baguley, ed., *Critical Essays on Émile Zola* (Boston:
G. K. Hall, 1986), pp. 60–4, and in *Documents of Modern Literary
Realism*, ed. George J. Becker (Princeton: Princeton University
Press, 1963), pp. 345–9.

'the Georgics of Filth': The *Georgics* is a poem in four books, probably
published in 29 BC, by the Latin poet Virgil. Its subject is farming
and rural life.

'with their history…': letter of 27 May 1886 to Jacques van Santen
Kolff, a Dutch critic and admirer of Zola's work.

'…all that is bodily': Mikhail Bakhtin, *Rabelais and his World*, trans.
Hélène Iswolsky (Bloomington and Indianapolis: Indiana
University Press, 1984), pp. 19–20, 21. 'The entire field of realistic
literature of the last three centuries', writes Bakhtin, 'is strewn with
the fragments of grotesque realism, which at times are not mere
remnants of the past but manifest a renewed vitality' (p. 24).

Chapter 9: After the *Rougon-Macquart*

'The child had come…': Émile Zola, *Doctor Pascal*, trans. Julie Rose,
ed. Brian Nelson (Oxford: Oxford University Press, 2020).

'Only then…': Émile Zola, *The Dreyfus Affair: 'J'accuse' and Other
Writings*, ed. Alain Pagès, trans. Eleanor Levieux (New Haven and
London: Yale University Press, 1996), p. 42.

Maurice Barrès, *Scènes et doctrines du nationalisme* (Paris: Félix
Juven, 1902), p. 44.

'There is only one issue…': *The Dreyfus Affair*, ed. Alain Pagès, p. 60.

Henry James, *Literary Criticism: French Writers, Other European
Writers, The Prefaces to the New York Edition*, ed. Leon Edel
(New York: Library of America, 1984), p. 885.

Henri Mitterand, 'The Scarlet Vision of the Revolution…', in Robert
Denommé and Roland Simon, eds, *Unfinished Revolutions:
Legacies of Upheaval in Modern French Culture* (University Park,
PA: Penn State University Press, 1998), pp. 43–63 (p. 60).

Jean Bedel, *Zola assassiné* (Paris: Flammarion, 2002).

Alain Pagès and Owen Morgan, *Guide Émile Zola* (Paris: Ellipses,
2002), pp. 172–80.

Further reading

Zola in English translation

All twenty volumes of *Les Rougon-Macquart*, as well as *Thérèse Raquin*, are available in Oxford World's Classics. Several novels (*Thérèse Raquin*, *The Drinking Den* (*L'Assommoir*), *Au bonheur des dames* (*The Ladies' Delight*), *The Earth*, *The Beast Within*, *The Debacle*) are available in Penguin Classics. *L'Assommoir* (London: Everyman, 1995) is a modernized version of Arthur Symons's 1894 translation; it is edited, with an introduction and a section on 'Zola and his Critics', by Nicholas White. *Pot-Bouille* (London: Everyman, 2000) is a modernized version of Percy Pinkerton's 1995 translation; it is edited, with an introduction and a section on 'Zola and his Critics', by Robert Lethbridge. *Germinal*, translated with notes by Raymond N. MacKenzie, and with an introduction by David Baguley, has been published by Hackett Publishing Company (Indianapolis, 2011). See also Emile Zola, *Looking at Manet*, with an introduction by Robert Lethbridge (London: Pallas Athene, 2013) and *The Dreyfus Affair: 'J'accuse' and Other Writings*, ed. Alain Pagès, trans. Eleanor Levieux (New Haven and London: Yale University Press, 1996).

Zola in French

Œuvres complètes, ed. Henri Mitterand et al., 20 vols (Paris: Nouveau Monde Editions, 2002–9).
Les Rougon-Macquart, ed. Henri Mitterand, 5 vols (Paris: Gallimard, Bibliothèque de la Pléiade, 1960–7).

Les Rougon-Macquart, ed. Colette Becker, 6 vols (Paris: Laffont, Bouquins, 1991–3).

Contes et nouvelles, ed. Roger Ripoll (Paris: Gallimard, Bibliothèque de la Pléiade, 1976).

Correspondance, ed. Bard H. Bakker et al., 10 vols (Montreal and Paris: Presses de l'Université de Montréal/Éditions du CNRS, 1978–95).

Carnets d'enquêtes: une ethnographie inédite de la France, ed. Henri Mitterand (Paris: Plon, 1986).

Écrits sur l'art, ed. Jean-Pierre Leduc-Adine (Paris: Gallimard, 1991).

Paperback editions of nearly all of Zola's individual texts exist in popular collections such as Folio, Classiques de Poche, and GF Flammarion.

Biographical studies

Frederick Brown, *Zola: A Life* (New York: Farrar, Straus, Giroux, 1995; London: Macmillan, 1996).

F. W. J. Hemmings, *The Life and Times of Emile Zola* (London: Elek, 1977).

Eileen Horne, *Zola and the Victorians* (London: MacLehose Press, 2015).

Michael Rosen, *The Disappearance of Emile Zola: Love, Literature and the Dreyfus Case* (London: Faber & Faber, 2017).

Philip Walker, *Zola* (London: Routledge & Kegan Paul, 1985).

Critical studies

Erich Auerbach, *Mimesis: The Representation of Reality in Western Literature*, trans. Willard R. Trask (Princeton: Princeton University Press, 1953), pp. 506–15.

David Baguley, *Émile Zola: L'Assommoir* (Cambridge: Cambridge University Press, 1992).

David Baguley, *Naturalist Fiction: The Entropic Vision* (Cambridge: Cambridge University Press, 1990).

David Baguley, ed., *Critical Essays on Emile Zola* (Boston: G. K. Hall & Co., 1986).

David F. Bell, *Models of Power: Politics and Economics in Zola's 'Rougon- Macquart'* (Lincoln, Nebr., and London: University of Nebraska Press, 1988).

William J. Berg and Laurey K. Martin, *Emile Zola Revisited* (New York: Twayne, 1992).

Harold Bloom, ed., *Emile Zola* (Philadelphia: Chelsea House, 2004).

Roger Clark, *Zola: L'Assommoir* (Glasgow: University of Glasgow French & German Publications, 1990).

Russell Cousins, *Zola: Thérèse Raquin* (London: Grant & Cutler, 1992).

Larry Duffy, *Le Grand Transit moderne: Mobility, Modernity and French Naturalist Fiction* (Amsterdam and New York: Rodopi, 2005), *passim*.

Lilian R. Furst, *L'Assommoir: A Working Woman's Life* (Boston: Twayne, 1990).

Lilian R. Furst and Peter N. Skrine, *Naturalism* (London: Methuen, 1971).

Kate Griffiths, *Émile Zola and the Artistry of Adaptation* (London: Legenda, 2009).

Anna Gural-Migdal and Robert Singer, *Zola and Film: Essays in the Art of Adaptation* (Jefferson, NC: McFarland & Co Inc, 2005).

Susan Harrow, *Zola: La Curée* (Glasgow: University of Glasgow French & German Publications, 1998).

Susan Harrow, *Zola, The Body Modern: Pressures and Prospects of Representation* (London: Legenda, 2010).

F. W. J. Hemmings, *Emile Zola* (second edition, Oxford: Oxford University Press, 1966).

F. W. J. Hemmings, ed., *The Age of Realism* (Brighton: The Harvester Press, 1978), esp. pp. 179–95.

Graham King, *Garden of Zola: Émile Zola and his Novels for English Readers* (London: Barrie & Jenkins, 1978).

John C. Lapp, *Zola before the* Rougon-Macquart (Toronto: University of Toronto Press, 1964).

Robert Lethbridge and Terry Keefe, eds, *Zola and the Craft of Fiction* (Leicester: Leicester University Press, 1990).

Harry Levin, 'Zola', in *The Gates of Horn: A Study of Five French Realists* (New York: Oxford University Press, 1963), pp. 305–71.

Valerie Minogue, *Zola: 'L'Assommoir'* (London: Grant & Cutler, 1991).

Henri Mitterand, *Émile Zola: Fiction and Modernity*, trans. and ed. Monica Lebron and David Baguley (London: The Émile Zola Society, 2000).

Brian Nelson, *Zola and the Bourgeoisie* (London: Macmillan, 1983).

Brian Nelson, ed., *Naturalism in the European Novel: New Critical Perspectives* (New York and Oxford: Berg, 1992).

Brian Nelson, ed., *The Cambridge Companion to Émile Zola* (Cambridge: Cambridge University Press, 2007).

Sandy Petrey, 'Nature, Society, and the Discourse of Class', in Denis Hollier, ed., *A New History of French Literature* (Cambridge, Mass.: Harvard University Press, 1989), pp. 774–80.

Patrick Pollard and Valerie Minogue, eds, *Rethinking the Real: Fiction, Art and Theatre in the Time of Emile Zola* (London: The Émile Zola Society, 2014).

Naomi Schor, *Zola's Crowds* (Baltimore: Johns Hopkins University Press, 1978).

Colin Smethurst, *Zola: Germinal* (London: Edward Arnold, 1974).

Caroline Snipes-Hoyt, Marie-Sophie Armstrong, and Riika Rossi, eds, *Rereading Zola and World-Wide Naturalism, Miscellanies in Honour of Anna Gural-Migdal* (Newcastle upon Tyne: Cambridge Scholars Publishing, 2013).

Hannah Thompson, *Naturalism Redressed: Identity and Clothing in the Novels of Emile Zola* (Oxford: Legenda, 2004).

Hannah Thompson, ed., *New Approaches to Zola: Selected Papers from the Cambridge Centenary Colloquium* (London: The Émile Zola Society, 2002).

Nicholas White, *The Family in Crisis in Late Nineteenth-Century French Fiction* (Cambridge: Cambridge University Press, 2006), *passim*.

Nicholas White, 'Naturalism', in William Burgwinkle, Nicholas Hammond, and Emma Wilson, eds, *The Cambridge History of French Literature* (Cambridge: Cambridge University Press, 2011), pp. 522–30.

Angus Wilson, *Émile Zola: An Introductory Study of his Novels* (revised edition, London: Secker & Warburg, 1964).

Zola

Index

For the benefit of digital users, indexed terms that span two pages (e.g., 52–53) may, on occasion, appear on only one of those pages.

Index